UNCOMFORTABLE GROWTH

Rick Williams

Dedication

To the people of Riverside Vineyard Church, past and present, who have faithfully journeyed with us.

*I am the vine; you are the branches.
If you remain in me and I in you,
you will bear much fruit;
apart from me you can do nothing.*

John 15:5

Copies of this book, including the Kindle version, can be purchased on Amazon.co.uk: http://Amazon.co.uk

© Copyright Rick Williams 2015

Unless otherwise indicated, all Scripture quotations are from THE HOLY BIBLE, NEW INTERNATIONAL VERSION®, NIV® Copyright © 1973, 1978, 1984 by Biblica, Inc.™ Used by permission. All rights reserved worldwide.

All rights reserved. No part of this publication may be reproduced, stored in a retrieval system or transmitted, in any form or by any means, electronic, mechanical, photocopying, recording, or otherwise, without the prior written permission of the copyright owners.

Cover design: Andy Black, Springetts

ISBN: 9781505726022

Contents

Dedication	2
Preface	6
Introduction	8
PART ONE – CULTURE	12
1. The Changing Culture and Spiritual Landscape	13
2. The Reshaping of the Church	28
3. Some Lessons from the Recent Past	39
PART TWO – THEOLOGY	55
4. God's Transformation of People	56
5. God's Mission in His World	79
6. God's Activity through His Church	93
PART THREE – PRACTICE	108
7. Jesus Made Disciples	109
8. Building a Disciple-Making Church	123
9. Leadership Culture	143
10. Churches that Develop Leaders	159
11. Planting Churches	176
12. Church Planting Reflections	190
Conclusion	213
Index of Subjects	219
Bibliography	221

Preface

The material in this book started life as a dissertation. The book version focuses upon how any church might engage with the realities and practices that make it more fully what it is called to be: God's people in the world for the sake of the world. The reflections on the Vineyard's experience in the United Kingdom are offered by way of illustration. It is therefore somewhat different from what I presented for the completion of my Doctorate of Ministry, at the School of Theology, Fuller Theological Seminary, in 2008. The title for the dissertation was "A Strategy for Planting Missional Vineyard Churches in the UK's Post-Christendom Culture". The reason for publishing in its present form is, in the first instance, to support and be a reference for a series of lectures to be given to the Vineyard Institute.

Let me make a number of comments up front. First, this is a book for the church and about the church. Although written from an experience within the Vineyard, it considers issues common to all churches. I hope lessons can be drawn which might be of benefit to all. Secondly, the book contains reflections upon the Vineyard Church in the UK and Ireland in general, and on the particular experience of Riverside Vineyard Church, which my wife Lulu and I planted and led, with the assistance of many gifted leaders, from 1988 to 2011. All of these reflections are very much a personal perspective, and are only tentative evaluations on some of our practices.

Conscious of my close proximity to immediate history, I make this offering fully realizing the need for what C.S. Lewis understood as "critical distance". This is a necessity if we are to be saved from the spirit and obsessions of our own times. I know that through ongoing learning others will continue to build on these thoughts both theologically and in practice.

Thirdly, and most importantly, I am only too aware of my own fallibility and am conscious that perspectives and lessons learnt have usually come through mistakes and the limitations in my own leadership, ministry and church. This is not therefore an attempt to paint our experience in glowing colours, but rather to point to God's amazing grace in using very ordinary people.

I am very grateful to those who read my draft, making comments and suggestions. They have helped to clarify expression and intent. There have been many rich conversations over the years from which insight and wisdom lodged in my mind, and which have now been expressed in writing. I am also conscious of the great gift I have received through authors and fine preachers and teachers. A great deal of them is found in these pages. But most especially I thank Lulu my wife for the many discussions, corrections and word-processing that she has done. She has been my patient and loving partner as we have sought to learn and serve through "uncomfortable growth" in ministry and church planting.

Introduction

Vineyards create the most stunning of cultivated landscapes. The rolling hills around Montalcino in Tuscany and the St. Emilion Estates in the Bordeaux are, to my mind, impossibly beautiful. From the old world to the new, these vistas are a paradise for our senses. Yet no cultivated land experiences such sharp change through the annual seasonal cycle, from vigorous green growth and burgeoning fruitfulness right through to the decimated appearance of winter, when all we see are amputated stumps devoid of any visible sign of life.

Little wonder that the Bible used the vineyard image to portray the heights and depths, joys and sadnesses of God's people. Isaiah presents us with a picture of idyllic purposefulness designed for great joy and celebration; "My loved one had a vineyard on a fertile hillside. He dug it up and cleared it of stones and planted it with the choicest vines. He built a watchtower in it and cut out a winepress as well" (Isaiah 5:1,2). Yet, just three verses later, the picture has entirely changed, "I will take away its hedge ... I will break down its walls, and it will be trampled. I will make it a wasteland, neither pruned nor cultivated, and briars and thorns will grow there" (Isaiah 5:5,6).

All of us involved in Christian ministry can, I think, relate

Introduction

to both these pictures; the unsurpassable fulfilment of kingdom ministry and the aching awareness of the church's frailness and vulnerability. This age-old tension is the subject of this book: *Uncomfortable Growth*. Everything about the Christian life contains the two realities of growth and discomfort; being a disciple, making disciples, being led, being a leader, developing leaders and planting churches. At the same time we are seeking to do so in a culture that tells us the opposite; growth, whether in the form of success, affluence or entitlement, is seen as a right that should come to us with ease. Jesus, however, points to a kingdom that is altogether different: the vine is pruned for fruitfulness, the seed of grain needs to fall and die in order to multiply.

In such a world, where does the church now find itself? What are the present challenges? Are they any different from what they have always been, or are there new realities to be considered?

The world is changing fast. It was in the 1960s that the singer/songwriter Bob Dylan assailed us with the lyrics, "You better start swimmin' or you'll sink like a stone/ for the times they are a-changin."[1] He was right! In fact we live in times when profound social change seems particularly turbulent and unrelenting. Graphically, and maybe prophetically, the chaotic changes seen in Western culture have parallels with disruption in nature. The gathering strength in air masses that spiral over oceans and continents associated with global climate change insists on capturing our attention. The depth and extent of the social and religious changes that have impacted the world are now becoming clear. The Christendom story no longer defines

---

[1] Bob Dylan, *The Times They Are A-Changin*, first released 1964 (Real Audio) Windows Media (56).

Western culture, yet the church has been perilously slow to adapt to the new realities.

There is little doubt that this is a huge challenge for the church, referred to by some as "adaptive challenge".[2] Adaptive challenges come from two possible sources: a significant threat, or a compelling opportunity, or indeed a combination of both. What are the major threats to the twenty-first century church? Might there also be unprecedented opportunities for it? Both are good reasons to stop, and re-evaluate God's essential call to the church, and to align our practices with that call.

Despite the enormity of cultural change the main areas of challenge for the church are not the external influences of shifting worldviews and attitudes. Rather, more than ever, the central locus for the people of God is to regain a fresh God-given consciousness of his calling and enablement. A dual task is required: the cultural engagement of the gospel through a "going" missional church on the one hand, and a radical transformation of believers as disciples of Jesus, on the other. We know that the church must go on changing without changing the timeless message of the gospel.

The book has three parts: Culture, Theology and Practice. In my own mind I picture the secular *Culture* as the soil in which we have been called to labour; *Theology* as the roots we must put down to provide secure anchorage for what we do; and *Practice* is what is seen above the surface, reflecting Jesus and his kingdom.

In Part One, the present cultural context for the church's mission is explored. In particular, Chapter 1 considers the impact and nature of the rapid cultural changes in society over

---

[2]Alan Hirsch, *The Forgotten Ways: Reactivating the Missional Church* (Grand Rapids: Brazos Press, 2006), 20.

recent decades. The church's response in reshaping herself is presented in Chapter 2. Chapter 3 draws some lessons for the church from the recent past, with reference to the experience of the Vineyard. What, from the culture, must we pay attention to? Are we listening too little or too much?

Part Two examines the Bible's grand narrative and mandate to provide a theological basis for the church and its mission. The next three chapters cover: the necessity of the believer's transformation (Chapter 4); questions relating to mission in a post-modern culture (Chapter 5); and the activity of the whole church, drawing inspiration from church planting (Chapter 6).

Part Three moves to practice and application. Two chapters are devoted to each of the following: making disciples (Chapters 7 and 8), developing leaders (Chapters 9 and 10) and the planting and developing of churches (Chapter 11 and 12). A fresh return to the Jesus of the gospels and his kingdom must be allowed to direct and reinvigorate the church and its mission.

PART ONE

CULTURE

CHAPTER 1

The Changing Culture and Spiritual Landscape

The biblical vision of human culture is vast and wonderful. It is complex, subtle and inescapable. However, every culture is a mixed bag of good and bad elements. It should not be a surprise, therefore, that the church cannot agree on how to respond to it.

It is difficult to think of a more divisive subject than how we, as Christians, relate to our post-modern world culture. Separation, engagement or indifference to it, are all championed. Like tectonic plates these perspectives are constantly on the move. Condemning, critiquing, copying or consuming are all responses identified by Andy Crouch, in his book, *Culture Making*.[3] He makes the important point that church movements have adopted different approaches to the culture at different times. The reason that all of these approaches are still with us is

---

[3]Andy Crouch, *Culture Making: Recovering Our Creative Calling* (Downers Grove, IL: InterVarsity Press, 2008).

that, at any given point in history, a particular response is felt necessary by the church, such as Bonhoeffer's condemnation of Naziism, or us condemning pornography. The church must think about which elements of the culture are good or bad, if it is not to uncritically imbibe the world's values.

My interest, in this book, is how we develop a unified biblical stance towards the world and its cultures, rather than spending too much time defining ourselves against other Christians, exaggerating the imbalance in others while becoming blind to our own. God's good news is for the world. Communicating that good news has been likened to the building of a bridge from the Bible to the contemporary world. God's unchanging message, for an ever-changing world. The Bible's message cannot be altered, but we must go on learning how to share that good news effectively in our culture. The bridge must therefore contain some two-way traffic. "We speak and listen, and speak and listen, and speak again, each time doing so more biblically, and more compellingly to the culture".[4]

From Incremental to Discontinuous Change

We live in a world experiencing unprecedented rates of change. Leonard Sweet states, "There is a new web page every two seconds, a new product every thirty seconds. World knowledge now doubles every eighteen months, with more new information having been produced in the last thirty years than in the previous five thousand"[5]. He goes on to observe, that with

---

[4]Timothy Keller, *Center Church: Doing Balanced, Gospel-Centered Ministry in Your City* (Grand Rapids, MI: Zondervan, 2012), 103.
[5]Leonard Sweet, *Aqua Church: Essential Leadership Arts for Piloting Your Church in Today's Fluid Culture* (Loveland, CO: Group Publish-

change happening so quickly it becomes increasingly challenging even to imagine the world of our parents or conceive the world of our children. Changes in culture are of course not new in themselves. What is new is the *rate* of change. William Easum describes this rate of change in terms of a transition from the Industrial Age to the Quantum Age[6]. The Industrial Age was a world of methodical, orderly change. Around the middle of the twentieth century, the rate of change began to increase in complexity and grow exponentially. Gone are the days of orderly, incremental change; we now experience chaotic, discontinuous change.

Cultural changes of this nature and magnitude are influencing every area of society including the church. Much has been observed and written about this. Eddie Gibbs and Ian Coffey describe the possibility of churches becoming so preoccupied by their internal problems that they fail to notice the "seismic proportions" of the cultural shift taking place in society at large.[7] Church leaders find themselves ministering in a world which often seems out of control, characterised by high levels of stress and uncertainty. As a consequence some may want to look to the church as a refuge from all this change, hoping that it will be one place where change does not take place. However, as John Henry Newman once astutely pointed out, if the church is to remain the same, it must change.[8]

---

ing Inc., 1999), 16.
[6]William M. Easum, *Sacred Cow Makes Gourmet Burgers* (Nashville: Abingdon Press, 1995), 19.
[7]Eddie Gibbs and Ian Coffey, *Church Next: Quantum Changes in Christian Ministry* (Leicester, England: Inter-Varsity Press, 2001), 24.
[8]Quoted in Alister E. McGrath, *The Future of Christianity* (Oxford, UK: Blackwell Publishers, Ltd., 2002), 73.

This has implications for Christian leadership. In previous centuries it was possible to engage in long term strategic planning because of society's stability or because change was predictable. Today, leadership and church communities increasingly need to be flexible and able to respond rapidly to change. Even so, far more is required than a rapid response. The church and the world are moving into uncharted territory where much of post-modern culture is, as yet, unmapped. But was this not also true for Abraham in the second century BC? "By faith Abraham, when called to go to a place he would later receive as his inheritance, obeyed and went, even though he did not know where he was going" (Hebrews 11:8).

As noted earlier, the chaotic changes seen in Western culture have parallels in nature. One of the features of living systems is the creative ability of organisms to renew themselves through disruptive change known as *autopoiesis*. I think this gives a hopeful analogy for the regeneration of the church – itself a living entity. Similarly, in organic chemistry disorder can paradoxically be the source of new order. So-called "dissipative structures" suffer loss as energy gradually ebbs away; but rather than leading to death of a system, it is part of the process of chemically reorganising into a form better suited to the demands of a changed environment. Chaos theory goes on to define a system as chaotic when it becomes impossible to know what it will do next. The system never behaves the same way twice. The paradox, however, is that if we look at such systems over time, they demonstrate an inherent orderliness. Throughout the universe order seems to exist within disorder and disorder within order.

Change is unsettling. It shakes the security of what is known. But Margaret Wheatley challenges the perception of change as a feared enemy.[9] She speaks of a paradoxical dance being observed in all of life; a dance of chaos and order, of change and stability. Here lies a creative perspective for viewing the church's role in a world experiencing massive change. Rather than an enemy, disorder and change can be the source of new order and growth.

Social and Spiritual Trends of the Last Forty Years

The huge social changes in Western culture find something of an explanation in both the macro and micro trends of the recent past. Further, what becomes apparent is that global trends are deeply connected with local circumstances and contexts.

Globalisation is a broad term with many meanings. In narrow economic terms, it signifies the increasing integration of economies across national borders through trade in goods and services, the migration of labour and the investment of capital.[10] Never has this sense of interconnectedness been more felt than in the recent financial crisis. We may quickly forget, but the global economy, by the spring of 2007, had come to resemble what Niall Ferguson described as, "an over-optimized electricity grid" – the financial equivalent of a blackout waiting to happen.[11]

New York Times columnist, Thomas Friedman, asks what

---

[9]Margaret J. Wheatley, *Leadership and the New Science: Discovering Order in a Chaotic World* (San Francisco: Berrett-Koehler Publishers, 1999), Chapter 1 and Chapter 8.
[10]Paul S. Mills, "Globalization and the World Economy," *Cambridge Papers* 14, no. 1 (2005): 1.
[11]Niall Ferguson, *Civilization: The West and the Rest* (London: Penguin Books, 2011), 301.

history will say (twenty years from now) was the most crucial development at the turn of the century.[12] Will it be the events of 9/11 and the Iraq war, or something entirely different, the convergence of technology and events that empowered China, India, and many other countries to become part of the economic success of globalization? For Friedman, cheap, ubiquitous telecommunications have finally removed all impediments to international competition, and with this "flattening" of the world there is doubt whether political systems will be able to adjust fast enough and in a sufficiently stable manner.

Global trends

The characteristics of globalisation can be distilled into a number of trends – all of which are felt locally to some degree.

1. *Radical migration.* At no time in history have we seen so much human movement, not always by choice. Millions of people are being displaced by poverty and war. The vast majority of these refugees are women and children. Whether migration is for these or for economic reasons, its impact is felt mostly at the local level. This often leads to contention over immigration policies.
2. *Urbanisation.* At the mid point of the last century, there were seven cities with a population of five million people. Today this number has risen to more than seventy. Despite people moving into cities to escape rural poverty, the chasm between rich and poor continues to grow at an alarming rate. Associated with both of these trends of migration and urbanisation is a third feature:

---

[12]Thomas L. Friedman, *The World is Flat: A Brief History of the Twenty-First Century* (New York: Farrar, Straus and Giroux, 2005).

3. *Population explosion.* Every second, four babies are born. Despite death from disease, war and famine, twice as many people are born each day, than die. About sixty years ago the global population reached its first billion. It took the entire history of mankind to accumulate that many people on the planet. Since that time a billion people have been added almost every decade. The global population in 2012 stood at 7.1 billion.[13] This massive rise in population has consequences for the environment. As a result of widespread environmental degradation many of the most vulnerable human beings suffer from the effects of flood, drought, and disease, and many more are uprooted and displaced.[14]
4. *Technology.* The Internet and social media have transformed our world through access to information, immediacy of communication, and their power to influence.
5. *Pluralism.* We must not assume that globalisation implies that we are moving towards a uniform culture. In fact as the world connects culturally and commercially it seems to become more divided religiously and ethnically.
6. *Post-Modern Thinking.* The optimism and scientific certainty that characterised much of modernity has increasingly given way to pessimism and ambiguity in its view of the world. In rejecting propositional certainty, postmodernism assumes truth is relative rather than ultimate, and is perplexed by revealed, unique truth.

---

[13]Erwin Raphael McManus, *An Unstoppable Force: Daring to Become the Church God Had in Mind* (Orange, CA: Yates & Yates, 2001), 47.
[14]Nick Spencer and Robert White, *Christianity, Climate Change and Sustainable Living* (London: Society for Promoting Christian Knowledge, 2007), 98.

National trends

While the population in the UK over the last forty years has risen by only 5% the number of households has increased by 31%, with an average of 2.4 people per household. Many people are choosing to live alone, are having children later on in life, or are single through relationship breakdown. At least 312 couples divorce every day, and 22% of children in England and Wales live in lone parent families.[15] There is inevitable pressure on available housing and many people are unable to get on to the housing ladder. Twenty-five percent of working men and 11% of working women work more than fifty hours a week. This is one of the highest rates in Europe.[16] Somebody calls the Samaritans every five seconds.

Andrew Marr, in his study of modern Britain, summed up recent history in this country as "the story of the defeat of politics by shopping." Margaret Thatcher's revolution shovelled away the rubble of the old state, and the consumer advanced. Far from it re-moralising the British with the Victorian values of frugality, saving, and orderliness, a conspicuous consumption has become the order of the day. This unprecedented consumerism has affected us all, as we are all too aware after the toxic loans and banking crisis of 2007/8. However, consideration for the poor, both nationally and globally, remains an emphasis in British society, as evidenced in things like Sport Relief, Children in Need and Overseas Government Aid.

New social structures have emerged, which have not replaced

---

[15]Church of England Report, *Mission-Shaped Church: Church Planting and Fresh Expressions of Church in a Changing Context* (London: Church House Publishing, 2004), 1–3.
[16]Ibid., 1–4.

neighbourhoods, but have changed them. As Martin Albrow comments, "The communities of the global age generally have no local centre. People living in the same street will have fleeting relationships with each other, having widely different lifestyles and household arrangements".[17] We relate to others through a variety of networks: workplace activities, baby and toddler groups, school and parent connections, leisure facilities and gyms, pubs and clubs.[18]

Spiritual trends

All of these social changes have coincided, perhaps unsurprisingly, with significant spiritual changes in the United Kingdom. These spiritual changes however are not always obvious. Listening to Professor Richard Dawkins, one might think that the country consisted largely of rampant atheism. Four days after the destruction of the World Trade Center in New York, Dawkins blamed the tragedy on something he called "religion". Religion, he suggested, is "a ready-made system of mind control which has been honed over centuries" and "teaches the dangerous nonsense that death is not the end."[19] He went on to claim, that by holding out the promise of an afterlife, religion devalues this life and makes the world "a very dangerous place."[20] It is understandable why a polemic like this against religion

---

[17] Martin Albrow quoted in Church of England Report, *Mission-Shaped Church*, 6.
[18] See Eddie Gibbs and Ryan K. Bolger, *Emerging Churches: Creating Christian Community in Postmodern Cultures* (London: SPCK, 2006), 24–26.
[19] Richard Dawkins, "Religions Misguided Missiles", *The Guardian* 15 (September 2001): 20.
[20] Ibid.

was published after the attack on the twin towers. Dawkins and others were, however, anxious to avoid charges of Islamophobia. Attacking Islam was taboo, but attacking religion per se was acceptable. Condemning one sixth of the world's population was irresponsible; incriminating three quarters of it was thought to be courageous. But this view is far from being widely held, as we will see later.

We are all too familiar with headlines trumpeting the "Dramatic Decline In Church Attendance" or "Church In Crisis". And certainly the statistics are not good. Sunday school attendance dropped from 55% to 4% of children during the twentieth century. Today in the United Kingdom, attendance averages 6.3% of the population. In the inner cities and amongst the young it is a good deal less. However, it would be wrong to conclude that the church in the UK universally resembles the BBC's amusing but woefully limited portrayal in its TV series, "Rev". I do not deny that ineffectual ministers and churches exist, but it is not the church that I, or many others, recognize.

Are We Becoming More Secular or More Religious?

Sociologist Peter Berger, writing in the New York Times in 1968 predicted that by "the twenty-first century, religious believers are likely to be found only in small sects, huddled together to resist a world-wide secular culture".[21] The widely held assumption of the mid-twentieth century was that secularisation was an irreversible process. However, thirty years later in 1999, Berger was writing about the "desecularisation of the world", observing that the world today was as furiously religious as it

---

[21] Peter Berger quoted in John Coffey, "Secularisation: Is It Inevitable?", *Cambridge Papers* 10, no.1 (March 2001): 1.

ever was and, in some places, even more so than ever.[22] However, secularism is a reality and has pushed determinedly to exclude Judeo-Christian moral precepts from civic life.

Yet despite the rapid de-Christianisation of Europe, the late twentieth century witnessed a dramatic resurgence of religion in many other parts of the world. The Islamic revolution in Iran and the rise of the Hindu National Party in India together with the resurgence of religion in the former territories of the Soviet Union can all be seen as reactions against the perceived imposition of a global secularised culture. Additionally, there has been the phenomenal spread of Pentecostalism, which from the humblest of beginnings in the first decade of the last century, grew explosively to become a world-wide movement of perhaps a quarter of a billion people.[23]

In the light of this, perhaps it should be asked whether Europe itself might be exceptional in its secularity? If European secularity is the result of a set of uniquely local circumstances, it would not necessarily be replicated elsewhere. Secularisation cannot predict the fate of religion in the modern world. As Coffey explains, "The prime effect of modernisation is not the decline of religion (secularisation), but the growth of religious and ideological plurality (diversification)."[24]

---

[22]Peter Berger, ed., *The Desecularization of the World: Resurgent Religion and World Politics* (Grand Rapids: Eerdmans, 1999).
[23]Harvey Cox, *Fire From Heaven: The Rise of Pentecostal Spirituality and the Reshaping of Religion in the Twenty First Century* (London: Cassel, 1996) referenced in McGrath, *The Future of Christianity,* 20.
[24]Coffey, *"Secularisation"* 3.

The Rise of Islam

Bishop Lesslie Newbigin, a few months before he died in 1998, was asked what he thought might be the significant missionary agenda for the Christian church in the early part of the twenty-first century. He replied, with characteristic clarity and prophetic insight, that he thought the first decade of the twenty-first century would be marked by "a major conflagration between militant Islam and the globalising tendencies of free market capitalism".[25] As I write there is no easy calm in the world, only vivid testimony to the violent nature of that conflagration. Isis (Islamic State) has burst on to the scene announcing the establishment of its Caliphate in Iraq and Syria. Almost daily, accounts of extreme brutality are reported. Young British Muslims leave this country to join the Jihad.

Alister McGrath traces the origins of the modern Islamic movement back to about 1875, when Jamal Al-Din al-Afghani urged Muslims to resist the growing Western influence in the Middle East by a reaffirmation of their Muslim heritage. The pre-Western golden Muslim age could be retrieved by a return to a personal religious piety, a reform and renewal of Islamic Shariah Law, and violent resistance to Western presence and influence.[26]

This represents a grim fundamentalism. The paradox of fundamentalism is that it depends upon secularism for its credibility. Karen Armstrong, in her book, *The Battle for God*, points out how fundamentalism and Western secular materialism exist

---

[25] Colin Greene, "Editorial," *The Bible in Transmission: A Forum for Change in Church and Culture*, Spring 2002, 3.
[26] McGrath, *The Future of Christianity*, 73–82.

in a symbiotic relationship.[27] Dislike of religious fundamentalism motivates the growth of secularism, which in turn generates a reaction leading to the swelling of fundamentalism.

Some writers see the fault lines of tomorrow's world lying along a diffuse and poorly understood line, dividing Islam from Christianity. Christianity is a growing presence in traditionally Islamic regions of the world such as Malaysia and Indonesia, while Islam has pushed south in Africa and has gained a presence in the West. Large Islamic communities have developed in Britain, where conservative Muslims colonize rather than integrate, in order to live by the Qur'an and Shariah Law. Rather than the world becoming increasingly homogenous, it is reminiscent of the Balkans, with territories divided along tribal and religious lines, rather than as nation states.

In order to understand the root causes of the rise of Islam, one needs to appreciate Islam's early history and sacred texts. Riddell and Cotterell argue that it is the Muslim world, and not the non-Muslim world, that stands at a crossroad. Islam has, throughout its history, contained elements of violence, legitimised by certain passages of the Qur'an, though put in question by other passages. For centuries, two streams within Islam, the violent stream and the stream advocating a more moderate approach to the non-Muslim world, have existed in constant tension. Only the Muslim world can ultimately deal with the roots of the problem.[28] This view stands in contrast to the popular current view, which places the burden of blame on the non-Muslim world in general and on the U.S. in particular.

---

[27]Karen Armstrong, *The Battle for God* (New York: Alfred A. Knopf, 2000).
[28]Peter G. Riddell and Peter Cotterell, *Islam in Context: Past, Present and Future* (Grand Rapids, MI: Baker Academic, 2003), 7–9.

What is to be the Christian response to all this? It feels overwhelming. But personally I am deeply encouraged by a couple, close friends of ours, who were powerfully converted to Christ from a Muslim background and who now reach out to Arabic speakers in different nations. Their approach is loving, straightforward and bold, always using Scripture to reveal the truth. We desperately need such courageous encouragement in the power of God's good news. We also take heart from the many accounts of Jesus being revealed to Muslims through visions and dreams.

Towards a Biblical Vision of Culture

Jesus deeply challenged the religious culture of his day, saying relatively little about the broader culture. His intention was that the former be salt and light to the latter. If the church is going to relate to the culture in any distinctively Christian way, we need to hold in mind the biblical vision of culture and whether it offers us some distinctive approaches.

The biblical vision is particularly captured in the first and last books of the Bible – two bookend accounts of the beginning and ending of human history. Genesis portrays the start of human culture in a Garden, which soon goes horribly wrong. Revelation portrays God's final fulfilment, not as a garden, but as a garden city; a new and holy city, where nature and culture blend in perfection. The rural beginnings of humanity have moved to an urban future. Here we see the city transformed from the site of sin and judgement, to the ultimate expression of grace: "The Holy City, the New Jerusalem, coming down out of heaven from God" (Revelation 21:2); a city where its river, trees and fruit are all giving life and healing to the nations

(Revelation 22:1–2). In between these biblical bookends, we have God's rescue worked out in human history.

From our vantage point we know very well that all cultures are complex, and interweave both positive and negative aspects. Residual sin in followers of Jesus means that the church is never nearly as good or distinctive as it should be; while common grace means that the world is never as bad as it could be. All human beings are both radically fallen, yet made in the likeness and image of God. By grace it is possible for all to be miraculously remade. Biblical teaching provides Christians in every age and culture with both boundaries and freedom to construct a godly approach. We know from the biblical vision that in the end there will be a great multitude that no-one can count from every nation, tribe, people and language standing before the throne and in front of the Lamb (Revelation 7:9).

CHAPTER 2

The Reshaping of the Church

Mid-twentieth century commentators largely failed to anticipate accurately the twenty-first century. As it has turned out, this is not an age of secular ideologies; it is an era of desecularisation. Our greatest challenge is deeply spiritual.

Towards the end of his book, *Civilization*, historian Niall Ferguson drops a depth charge into his analysis. He quotes a member of the Chinese Academy of Social Sciences, part of a team tasked with discovering the reason for the West's prominence over the last 500 years. They had been asking whether the West's success was because of its military prowess, or the result of its economic or political systems? They concluded that it was none of these – rather it was due to Christianity and the societal values it creates.[29] According to this conclusion, the West is losing the very thing that once made it great – its faith and Christian values – whilst China, the world's fastest growing economy, is discovering it.

---

[29]Ferguson, *Civilization*, 287.

How is the church in the West responding to the fast changing culture and religious landscape? A reshaping of the church is taking place. This reshaping can be viewed historically from three particular successive vantage points.

The Church at the Centre

For centuries, Christianity enjoyed a dominant and privileged place in our national life, yet the church today no longer shapes public discourse as it once did. The fourth and the twentieth centuries form a framework for the Constantinian view of Christianity. Since the conversion of the Roman Emperor Constantine in A.D. 313, until approximately the mid-point of the twentieth century, the church occupied a central position within Western societies.

Following Constantine's conversion, Christianity moved from being a marginalised, and persecuted movement gathering secretly in houses and catacombs, to being the favoured and sponsored religion of the Empire. This began a period of history when the church assumed influence by its connection to temporal and secular powers. Christendom's high water mark occurred in the Middle Ages and continued into the 1700s. Since the emergence of the Enlightenment it has been in decline.

In the last century, what the Vietnam War did to the American psyche in the 1960s and 1970s, the First World War did for Europe, but on a much larger scale. However, the Christendom view still remains, peculiarly, a primary definer of the church's self-understanding in much of the UK. This view of the church in society is represented in Figure 1.[30]

---

[30] Eddie Gibbs, Class Lecture Notes from "Growing Churches in a

Uncomfortable Growth

Figure 1. The Traditional Society: Church at the Centre

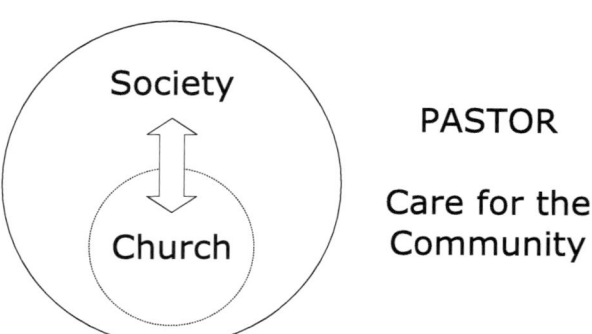

In the United Kingdom such a society had strong rural origins with the clergyman seen as a chaplain to the whole community. He would officiate at the various rites of passage, and members of that society were assumed to be Christian by birth rather than by choice. The church building, invariably situated in a central location, would symbolise the Christian religious presence in that community. Though people were "Christianised" by the Christendom culture, they were not necessarily regenerated or converted with the gospel.

Care needs to be taken with the language of Christendom. It is a large word, with broad associations. I am using it primarily in the sense of how the church sees itself and its influence in the world. When Christendom was well established, the church could assume that the institutions of the culture went a considerable way towards giving citizens the basic "mental furniture" for understanding Christianity. The message of the Christian

---

Post-Christendom World", Topic 9, Fuller Theological Seminary, 2005, 101.

faith was largely seen as credible and positive. Gospel presentations could be kept rather simple, stressing the importance of repentance and faith, without the huge work of having to establish the very existence of the biblical God. But all this has changed, "The world that Christians in the West had known – where the culture tilted in the direction of traditional Christianity – no longer existed".[31] As the main cultural institutions stopped supporting Christianity, Christians felt inevitably out of place in their own society.

Oliver O'Donovan points out that while there may be some problems with the excesses of Christendom creating a sense of privilege and entitlement in the church, it did produce much that was thoroughly good.[32] Further, we live in a society that wishes to forget that Christian heritage. The idea that there was once a pure form of Christianity that existed before Constantine, which can somehow now be recovered, is naive. This Restoration Theology comes in many forms, and too readily dismisses the significance of historic Christianity that has shaped the church. That the church has to adapt missionally in response to massive shifts in culture seems obvious, but historic continuity is also necessary for the process of dynamic change among the people of God.

Philip Jenkins argues in *The Next Christendom* that the history of Christianity is a history of innovative adaptations.[33] The book takes a thorough look at the changing face of Christianity, both geographically (shifting firmly to the southern

---

[31] Keller, *Center Church*, 183.
[32] Oliver O'Donovan, *The Desire of the Nations: Rediscovering the Roots of Political Theology* (Cambridge University Press, 1996).
[33] Philip Jenkins, *The Next Christendom: The Coming of Global Christianity* (Oxford University Press, 2002).

Uncomfortable Growth

hemisphere), and theologically (increasingly conservative and embracing the supernatural). The effects of this on global politics, Jenkins argues, will be enormous, as religious identification begins to take precedence over allegiance to secular nation-states. His conclusion is that there is one overarching lesson from the changing fortunes of the church. Whether one looks backward or forward in history, one sees that "Christianity demonstrates a breathtaking ability to transform weakness into strength".[34]

When a Christendom "mindset" persists, it subtly limits the church from acting in biblical ways. The focus tends to become that of preserving the church, which stifles bold and creative outreach. It is this mindset, rather than a particular reading of history, that needs God's renewal.

Three limiting practices are perpetuated as a consequence.[35]

1. Instead of becoming more incarnational (us going into the world) the church remains largely attractional (you come to us), primarily concerned with maintaining and serving its flock.
2. Rather than a "whole-of-life" spirituality, a dualistic separation of life and faith emerges, which may give colour to our private lives, but which has little public impact. Rodney Clapp is particularly critical of this form of Christianity, arguing that such privatised faith is in fact *gnosticism*, and that such religion is not Christi-

---

[34] Philip Jenkins, *The Next Christendom: The Coming of Global Christianity* (Oxford University Press, 2002), 220.
[35] Michael Frost and Alan Hirsch, *The Shaping of Things To Come: Innovation and Mission for the 21st-Century Church* (Peabody, MA: Hendrickson Publishers, 2003), 12.

anity at all.[36] He sees the retreat of Christianity into the private individual sphere as a "kind of Constantinian retrenchment".[37]

3. The mode of leadership often remains hierarchical, status-conscious and lacking sufficient focus on equipping the people for the work of ministry. These limitations have a significant effect on the church's mission.

Moving on now from the church being at the centre of society (AD 313 to mid-twentieth century), we see the church becoming increasingly marginalised in the world.

The Church Marginalised

Henri Nouwen writes that Christians still long to "touch the centre" of men's and women's lives but now find themselves on the "periphery, often pleading in vain for admission."[38] They are no longer "where the action is, where the plans are made and the strategies are discussed."[39] As the twentieth century went on, the church found itself increasingly pushed from the centre of society to the margins, with its natural influence diminishing. This church of modern society is depicted in Figure 2.

---

[36] Rodney Clapp, *A Peculiar People: The Church as Culture in a Post-Christian Society* (Downers Grove, IL: InterVarsity Press, 1996), 34–36.

[37] Ibid., 43.

[38] Henri J.M. Nouwen, *The Wounded Healer* (Garden City, NY: Image/Doubleday, 1979), 86–87.

[39] Ibid.

Figure 2. Modern Society: Church Marginalised[40]

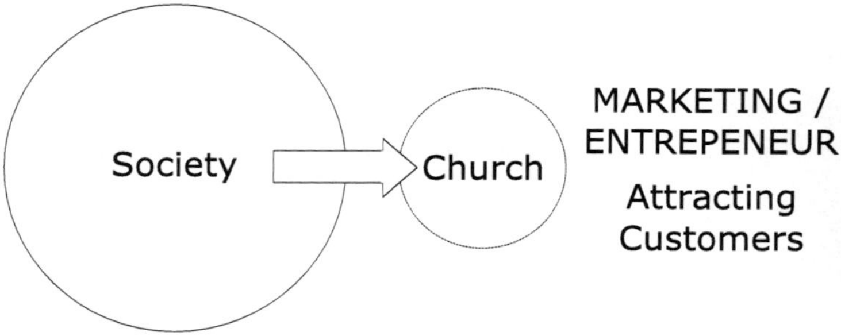

Society → Church

MARKETING / ENTREPENEUR
Attracting Customers

The optimism that characterised much of modernity was reflected in sections of the church. For example, one response to this new situation was to think in entrepreneurial terms. Marketing strategies in the modern consumer society seek to identify the unfulfilled wants and needs of population segments. Realising that Christianity is increasingly dislocated from society, the church has looked at ways of attracting "customers".

The centralised church of the traditional society was replaced by a de-centred church catering, in some instances, to specific personal needs. This was done through various organisational techniques, marketing strategies and entrepreneurial leadership. It sees its mission in terms of attracting people from society to the church. However, the gospel is not a product developed for a restricted market. Marketing runs the risk of turning the gospel message into a means of attaining some kind of personal fulfilment. The gospel, is not a message to attract customers, but God's gift to repentant sinners.

Nevertheless, many church marketing strategies have

---

[40] Gibbs, "Growing Churches in a Post-Christendom World", Topic 9, 101.

undoubtedly been motivated by mission. And we have needed it. In the seven years, 1998 to 2005, the church in the UK "lost" half a million people – a depressing thought when it is in the business of "finding" people.[41] Those utilising this entrepreneurial approach felt that not to do so was to be missionally inactive. Nevertheless, frustration has been expressed at this "attractional" model of church. The root of the objection is not the idea that a church should be unattractive, or abandon all its programmes, but that its priority should be to equip and mobilise the people of God to *go* into the world.

This is an unfair criticism of churches that are able to attract healthy numbers of pre-Christians. Clearly there are churches that appear to be highly programmatic and attractional, and yet which manage to draw significant numbers of people who then interact with the gospel and its implications. This underlines the reality that gospel ministry can interface with many models of church while retaining a missionary effectiveness.

We turn now to see how the marginalised church can rediscover its call to "go" into the society of the twenty-first century.

The Church Infiltrating

In this quickly changing world, the church must have the ability and flexibility to engage with the world and carry out effective mission. This is the third vantage point from which to see a reshaping of the church.

A good deal of experimentation is taking place in order to learn what a post-modern expression of faith and church looks

---

[41] Peter Brierley, *Pulling out of the Nosedive: A Contemporary Picture of Churchgoing: What the 2005 English Church Census Reveals* (London: Christian Research, 2006).

Uncomfortable Growth

like. This requires very careful thought, as it is surely easier to deconstruct the church than to reconstruct her.[42] Nevertheless, we have to face the reality that the church must continue to change in order to become missionally engaging. The essence of the contemporary church is expressed in Figure 3.

Figure 3. Post-Modern Society: Church Infiltrating.

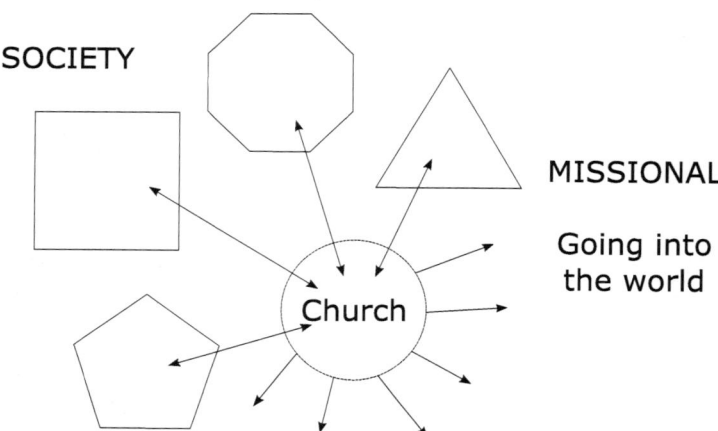

The orientation and movement of the infiltrating church reverses the approach of the church in traditional and modern societies. Rather than expecting the world to come to the church, we are to equip the church to go into every diverse segment of society, in order to live and proclaim the kingdom.

These are foundational rather than superficial changes, and require courage. Stanley Hauerwas and William Willimon see a fundamental issue in whether the church can be faithful to

---

[42]A further discussion of this can be found in Gibbs and Bolger, *Emerging Churches*, 27–46.

its peculiar vision of what it means to live and act as disciples.[43] Their concern is that "the world has tamed the church" and the church does not know it.[44] The Christians of the New Testament shaped their character and way of life in the image of their God. The world of that day demanded that Caesar was Lord: the church responded publicly that "Jesus was Lord". This points us to the essential issues of Christology, missiology and ecclesiology, which are considered in Part Two.

Church history makes us aware how tenuous the life of the church has been on occasions. At the time of the collapse of the Roman Empire, for example, when troops were withdrawn from Britain, the church in Britain faced virtual extinction. On that occasion, the church that then existed played a relatively small part in creating the new church that was to come. It seems to have had little ability to adapt and change. Instead, God used the missionary zeal of the Celtic Christians together with missionaries from Rome.

The church today needs to recover its "sent-ness". It is to be a sent and going church, a movement of God through his people, sent to bring the gospel to a broken world. The emphasis is incarnational, whereby God's people "go and dwell", being the light and salt of Jesus' kingdom in every sphere of life. Yet church leaders in the West have little or no missiological training. Devoid of the instinct to think like a missionary and ask missiological questions, many often default to methodologies and programmes.

---

[43] Stanley Hauerwas and William H. Willimon, *Resident Aliens: Life in the Christian Colony, A Provocative Christian Assessment of Culture and Ministry for People Who Know That Something is Wrong* (Nashville: Abingdon Press, 1989), 39.
[44] Ibid., 41.

Uncomfortable Growth

It is not easy to live in a society that is increasingly distanced from the Christian faith. But we cannot shy away from the world, which God has called us to love and serve. We have the supreme model for this in Jesus Christ himself. He came into the world and lived among us. When he went to the cross he became subject to injustice, suffering and weakness – all the things that we face. The cross lovingly confronts us with our own sin and lostness, and that of the world, from which nothing less than the death of Jesus can save us. He sought and found us, and now sends us back into the world with his life.

Many church leaders are taking these challenges seriously and experimenting with missional initiatives. Not all of these have resulted in health and growth. Style sometimes rises above substance. But the church needs to continue exploring this vital thinking and experimentation in order to be reshaped for God's kingdom opportunities in the UK and beyond.

CHAPTER 3

Some Lessons from the Recent Past

The church has certainly tried a lot of things! It has not been idle at suggesting new ways of reshaping itself: Emergent, Fresh Expressions, purpose driven, seeker sensitive, cell church, messy church, simple church, liquid church, organic church, deep church, total church, centre church! I'm sure there are things to learn from all of them. If a new church is required for a new world, what does that look like? What is the "newness" that the Bible speaks of? Might we be captured by the wrong kind of newness, and discover that the church's agenda has been hijacked? These are all questions to which we will return in later chapters.

Church planting is a missional response to Jesus' instruction to take his good news into all the world. It is one way to go and infiltrate in a changing, post-modern world. The relevance of church planting may not be immediately obvious to everyone, but the missional impulse that inspires church planting is the same impulse that every missionally concerned church knows. I think there are lessons for us all from the experience of church planting in the recent past.

Church Planting Across the UK

In the 1990s, an attempt was made to engage in saturation church planting, using the DAWN strategy (Disciple A Whole Nation). The suggested name was Challenge 2000 and a goal of planting 20,000 new congregations by the year 2000 was adopted at the first DAWN Congress in February 1992. Virtually every denomination and stream in the UK was present.

There were, however, significant problems that flowed from the adoption of this goal. An unreasonable focus on the Millennium (less than eight years away) left insufficient time to experiment and learn from what was, for many, the relatively new experience of church planting. The largely universal report from denominations was that their church planting goals were hopelessly underachieved, leading to demoralisation and a loss of confidence and energy. By the late 1990s the goal of planting 20,000 new churches had slipped quietly away.[45] A survey of church planting noted a decline in activity in the second half of the 1990s, before a resurgence of interest since 2000.[46]

During this time, the experience of church planting streams was different from mainline denominations. New Frontiers, for example, had already committed their network to ongoing church planting, and is on record as indicating that the Challenge 2000 initiative helped to give legitimacy to their activity.

The disappointment of Challenge 2000 was not, however, the end of the story. Out of the limelight, and not possessing its previous profile, the church planting process had begun

---

[45] For a more detailed account, see Martin Robinson, *Planting Mission Shaped Churches Today* (Oxford: Monarch Books, 2006), 21–29.
[46] George Lings and Stuart Murray, *Church Planting, Past, Present and Future* (Cambridge: Grove Evangelism 61, 2003), 25.

to receive deeper reflection. Church planting critiques, such as that by Stuart Murray, analysed and re-evaluated this particular strategy.[47] Hard questions were asked and evaluated by listening to the critics of church planting. Questions such as: Has church planting become an end in itself rather than a means to an end? Has the obsession with methodologies clouded and distorted the biblical understanding of the mission of the church? This re-evaluation has led to asking even more fundamental questions: What is the essence of Christianity? What is the church? and What is its mission? These "what" questions have pressed some into looking again at the church's theological framework (see Part Two). Out of this, the more practical "how" questions, rightly valued by practitioners, can be explored.

In his book, *Planting Mission Shaped Churches Today,* Dr. Martin Robinson suggests that there are at least five good reasons for taking church planting seriously.[48]

1. Populations are not static. New housing in new locations, and high levels of immigration, are a prominent feature of the UK.
2. Church planting is necessary for the life-cycle of churches. Not all churches live forever, and there is a need for replacement by birthing new churches.
3. Church planting is a natural part of the redefining of the overall make-up of the church. Whether one notices it or not, the "centre" of church life is constantly changing and God may choose to use, at times, some unlikely vehicles.

---

[47] Stuart Murray, *Church Planting: Laying Foundations* (Carlisle, Cumbria: Paternoster Press, 1998).
[48] Robinson, *Planting Mission Shaped Churches Today*, 30, 31.

4. Church planting offers an opportunity to experiment. Treating church activities as provisional, and experimental, is necessary for fresh engagement with the world.
5. Many of the disciplines contained within church planting can be applied to existing churches as part of a revitalisation process in mission. There is a need to resurrect a mission ethos in existing churches, as well as to plant many new congregations.

Mike Breen's work with "missional communities" deserves comment. "Missional communities" are called different things in different places but the idea is much the same.[49] The defining focus is on reaching a specific neighbourhood or network of relationships, and this mission is the glue for togetherness. The group can be a new church plant or (more commonly) a subset of a larger church. A number of features define the missional communities that Breen and others have seen established.

1. Particular attention is given to mid-sized communities of 20–50 people, but no more than 70. The idea is that this number of people resembles the benefits of an extended family, neither so small as to become entirely self-focussed, nor so large as to become missionally lazy or unengaged.
2. The missional life is to be worked out together in community with the sharing of three distinct dimensions of "up", "in" and "out" (relationship with God, one another and the neighbourhood). Missional communities need a balanced expression of these three dimensions in order to be healthy, growing communities.

---

[49]See Mike Breen and Alex Absalom, *Launching Missional Communities: A Field Guide* (Myrtle Beach, S.C.: Sheriar Press, 2010).

3. A "huddle" (a group of 4–12 current or future leaders) is the vehicle for discipling and training in the community. It meets every 1–2 weeks, and is led by a seasoned leader who intentionally trains those in the group. The leadership role involves coaching and accountability.

A friend once said to me, while discussing the possibility of this book, "Write about what you know". I think it was good advice. My own experience of church planting is within the Vineyard family of churches, and it is to this we now turn.

The Vineyard and Church Planting

The influence of the Vineyard in the United Kingdom began in the early 1980s. This influence related largely, although not exclusively, to renewal in the mainline churches. The influence and significance of this God-quickened renewal has been far-reaching and documented.[50] The New Wine network, Soul Survivor, Holy Trinity Brompton (HTB) and the ALPHA Course, Mike Breen's missional work in Sheffield and beyond, all acknowledge the primary influence of Vineyard ministry in their developing mission. During these years church networks such as New Frontiers International and Pioneer were also enthusiastic partners and participants. A spirit of co-operation

---

[50] Such documentation includes: Bill Jackson, *The Quest for the Radical Middle: A History of the Vineyard* (Cape Town, South Africa: Vineyard International Publishing, 1999); John Wimber with Kevin Springer, *Power Healing* (London: Hodder & Stoughton Limited, 1986), Appendix D: David C. Lewis, *Signs and Wonders in Sheffield: A Social Anthropologists' Analysis;* A variety of contributors, *Riding the Third Wave: What Comes After Renewal?*, ed. Kevin Springer (London: Marshall Pickering, 1987).

was sown which continues today.

Faithful to Christian orthodoxy, with an expectation of the supernatural, the Vineyard's simplicity was seen as adaptable to different contexts. In addition, the ability to readily reproduce itself meant that there were the almost inevitable ingredients for a Vineyard church planting contribution in the United Kingdom. Four Vineyard churches were finally planted in the late 1980s with the conviction that they were called to initiate a church planting movement that would partner with the renewal and mission of the existing church in the UK.

These church planting efforts were influenced by missiologists like Roland Allen who drew on the experience of the majority world to articulate a missionary model for Western church leaders.[51] Church planting, for him, was to be self-financing, self-governing, and self-reproducing. As a consequence, the Vineyard church planting model was based on leaders being bi-vocational and not dependent on outside financing. It was a high risk, low security venture. The object was to go into the culture, interact with it, and find ways of expressing the kingdom of God that would touch people's lives. As the initial church plants took root and grew, a platform for training and releasing new church plants developed, under the leadership of John and Ele Mumford, so that by the end of 2010 there were around one hundred Vineyard churches in the UK and Ireland. (An analysis of this church planting experience can be found in Chapter 12.)

---

[51] See for example Roland Allen, *Missionary Methods, St. Paul's or Ours?* (Grand Rapids, MI: Eerdmans, 1962).

Reflections on the Vineyard's Experience

What lessons can be learnt from the Vineyard's brief history and experience? Movements, like individual churches, cannot do everything, and it is a mistake to try. There can also be a subtle pressure to become like others, where distinctives are diminished. Rather, by being ruthlessly true to whom God has called and enabled us to be, we become the greatest blessing we can be, to the body of Christ and the world. Like any other network of churches, we are at our best when we focus on being faithful to what God has given and shown.

The Vineyard's strengths, if we can call them that, are certainly not exclusive to us, or in any way dependent on us. They are gifts of God's grace and accessible to all followers of Jesus. But our history and circumstances do allow us to express these contributions in particular ways for the benefit of others. What, then, would the last 25 years indicate are the distinctives to which we must remain true, and continue to give away to the body of Christ?

A supernatural expression of Jesus' ministry

The explosion of writing on the kingdom of God in recent years has frequently ignored or stripped the kingdom of its supernatural dimension. Social justice issues, such as modern day slavery through human trafficking, and care for the environment, are urgent issues of the kingdom of God. But let us never retreat from the miraculous dimension of Jesus' ministry that so clearly makes conversion, healing the sick and dealing with the demonic, Christ's liberating mark.

We remember that Jesus came as the anointed Warrior-King to re-establish God's rule by plundering Satan's kingdom (1

John 3:8 c.f. Mark 1:23–28). Jesus' ministry of word and deeds demonstrated repeatedly the nature of God's present and coming kingdom – a place where the brokenhearted, condemned, sinful, oppressed and sick found salvation (Luke 4:18–21). To pull away from this supernatural aspect of Jesus' ministry, on the basis of thinking that by doing so we are more appealing to our culture, is astonishing. Our world needs Jesus and the power of His ministry. We must continue to humbly explore and grow in this treasured discovery and gift.

The worship of God and a thirst for his presence

New songs and hymns of worship are springing up from all manner of places within the body of Christ. The Vineyard has played a part in that enrichment of Christian worship and experience. I remember years ago travelling through the dusty, hot streets of Kampala, Uganda, and hearing a Vineyard worship song rising above the hubbub of everyday life.

We, along with the rest of the church, need to go on valuing and deepening the experience of worship. We understand that worship through music is not the sum total of worship, but those experiences of worship through song and the grateful awareness of God's presence, provide platforms for our whole lives to be an act of worship to God.

Together with the God-given understanding that comes from preaching, teaching and living out God's word, the presence of God expands our awareness of God's majestic awe. Time and again in that place of worship we return to experience God's unconditional love and forgiveness, as well as His burning holiness and justice that quickens our desire to be pleasing to Him. Our reward is for God to be glorified. It is about Him and His glory, not about us and our recognition.

The awareness of God's presence quickens our understanding and motivation that we are living every moment before an all-seeing, all-hearing God. Worship is an opportunity to consecrate ourselves afresh and to resist the incessant temptation to turn even the good things in our lives into ultimate things. These are idols, which must give way to the Lordship of Jesus so that He has the whole of our lives.

A sound theological foundation

John Wimber's ground-breaking teaching and ministry was, for many of us, made intelligible and yes, thrilling, by its significant grappling with the ministry of Jesus recorded in the gospels. Karl Barth, the great Swiss theologian, warned us not to make any biblical theme the focus of Scripture, other than the name of Jesus Christ. Christ alone unifies all Scripture. When we look at the word of God from the perspective of the centrality of Jesus, we realize that the message and ministry of Jesus are inseparably linked to the kingdom of God.

This unifying and inspiring biblical lens has been tremendously significant for the Vineyard's mission, as it must be for the mission of the church generally. It enriches our worship of God as King; it quickens faith and boldness to step out in the present and follow our Lord who is able to do the impossible; it humbles us time and again as we suffer and experience the disappointments which are the inevitable realities of this age, and as we long for Christ's return and wait for the completion of his kingdom. It takes us into the Bible's grand narrative, God's meta-story encompassing creation, the fall, redemption, going to the nations and a new heavens and earth. It is this good news kingdom that we see Jesus demonstrating and declaring to the lost, poor and broken – and we must do no less.

A contextualised expression of church

A significant feature of the founding Vineyard churches in the late 1970s in North America was how well attuned and accessible they were to contemporary culture. Here were churches that were inventive, flexible and reaching hordes of people. During this early period the Vineyard expression of church was well attuned to Western culture. However, since that time the world has continued to distance itself from the church in unprecedented rates of social change. A fair critique may well be that we have not kept pace with these changes.

As a movement becomes more established, we are told that it will find itself gravitating to the security, but inflexibility, of institutionalism. The language of denominationalism is not helpful in our culture as it raises centralised and institutional issues, where policies rather than people are emphasised. To flourish, a movement will know that leadership exists to serve churches on the ground, rather than churches believing they exist to support the "denomination". We must resist institutional drift and aim to "travel lightly" in our mission. This will encourage experimentation and risk-taking together with streamlined and relational procedures.

The mobilisation of every disciple

Leaders are to be trainers, and the people are the disciple-makers. I remember John Wimber's extraordinary gift in being able to instruct and practically mobilise crowds of would-be disciples into effective ministers of Jesus' ministry. At a practical level in church life, there is little else that is as important as this key distinctive of insisting that all believers are ministers. This characteristic of Christian life is always under threat.

The history of the church indicates the pervasive movement from functional to positional ministry. It is a drift towards "churchy" things, even a subtle clericalism in attitudes and practice. In fact it is believed that for the first couple of hundred years of history the church had no clergy. Rather it was made up of believers and leaders who seemed to have clearly understood that they were all being sent on a mission by the Lord Jesus Christ. This release of ministry includes the call to plant new churches. It is not just the multiplication of ministry through individual members that we must insist on, but also the freedom to equip and release those who will multiply that same releasing ministry in and through new church plants.

In the final chapter, the potential for future growth in the Vineyard and the church generally, is explored.

One Church's Experience: Riverside Vineyard Church

Riverside Vineyard Church (RVC) is located on the west side of London and is a fifteen minute drive south-east of Heathrow International Airport. The church was planted in 1988 by my wife Lulu and me, and a handful of very committed people. RVC's story is neither one of spectacular ministry nor exceptional growth. We have neither been a vehicle for revival nor grown into a mega church.

However, no church is entirely ordinary. Every one has its own specific characteristics, even personality and calling. RVC has had extraordinary people who have exercised gifts faithfully to ensure that the church's core ministries of worship, preaching and outreach have been done with consistency and to the very best of its gifts and energy. Three further features have shaped RVC as a church.

Church planting

Being one of the original church plants, RVC had a strong sense of call and vision to reproduce churches. In fact, its vision centred around planting a church that would plant churches. We came to the view, that in our context and with this vision, having a church of around 500 people that regularly reproduced new churches, would be more effective than seeking to grow endlessly in size ourselves. This conclusion also seems to be supported by Natural Church Development research where the growth and mobilisation rates of church members decrease with increasing church size.[52]

To this end, we allocated resources and intentionally trained potential church planters, so that between 1994 and 2006 we were able to send out on average one new church plant every year. Lessons from this experience are discussed in Chapter 12. Following a venue project beginning in 2003, the church centre is now located on a redeveloped printing factory site in the heart of Feltham. This centre has been consciously built as a multi-purpose auditorium for 500 with adjoining facilities to pursue an equipping and going strategy.

Ethnic diversity

Like any church, RVC has sought to explore the opportunities for ministry in its locality. The area is densely populated and ethnically diverse, and historically has accommodated largely manual workers and lower-middle class people. Recent congregational surveys show over thirty-five different nationalities

---

[52] Christian A. Schwarz, *Natural Church Development Handbook: A Practical Guide to a New Approach* (Bedford, UK: British Church Growth Association, 1998).

in regular attendance, and up to 50% of the congregation at some services coming from a non Anglo-Saxon background. This diversity has contributed to a richness of church community life and pointed the way to some outreach ministries, such as classes that teach English as a foreign language.

Communities rarely stay the same. A redevelopment programme in the centre of Feltham has provided new homes and retail outlets. With its good transport links and developing leisure facilities, it is now attracting an increasing number of young professionals into the newly built apartments. The close proximity to Heathrow International Airport has spawned hostels for asylum seekers waiting for their cases to be processed, and the holding of detainees in Colnbrook Detention Centre. These have both provided further avenues for outreach ministry.

Mission

From the outset of the church our conviction was that God would give us opportunities, not just locally, but also nationally and overseas. To help understand the local needs, a survey was conducted. The people most in need were identified as youth (12–16 years), with a distinct lack of community facilities, and the elderly. This gave us some specific information that informed our ministry. Storehouse, a ministry providing good quality clothing, equipment and food to those in need, has become a major part of the church's life and identity. Our contribution nationally has focused mainly on sending out church plants, located as far afield as St. Andrews in the north, and Bournemouth in the south. Mission abroad is increasingly being shaped by RVC people who desire to contribute back into their countries of origin. Mission work in East and West Africa, and Bulgaria are all evolving through this source. Other mission partnerships involve France and Thailand.

In 2011, Lulu and I transitioned the Senior Leadership of RVC to Andy and Bethan Chapman, who now lead the church as Senior Pastors. As in any such transition, the incoming leaders require complete freedom to determine the ongoing vision and emphasis of the church. Andy and Bethan continue to strongly centre the church around an outward looking vision, and welcome and celebrate ethnic diversity.

To Sum Up

Church models come and go. The real challenge, irrespective of labels and categories, is to pattern our missional practices on Jesus: his life, his gospel, and his kingdom. The missional challenge of bringing the good news to an estranged society is the calling of every church. Church planters acutely know this challenge because the plant dies unless mission happens.

Today, we live in a world where the culture no longer accords Christianity special treatment. Might this not be a good thing? Released from any automatic sense of responsibility to support the *status quo*, the church can again concentrate on simply being the followers of Jesus. Rather than being a "moral majority" the church can, once again, be a "prophetic minority", going to and serving the world.

Opportunities abound for churches that will boldly engage with the culture and its diverse ideologies. We have an excellent environment for evangelism. God calls us to live humbly, yet distinctively, inviting others to consider God's good news.

Discussion Questions on Culture

1. It has been said that followers of Jesus Christ confront, in the modern world, the most powerful culture in human history ... the world's first truly global culture. What particular characteristics are "powerful" and where do the opportunities and warnings lie? Do we listen too little or too much to the culture? For study: Luke 12:13–21.
2. Three different interactions of the church with the world are presented in Figures 1, 2 and 3. Which model most clearly describes your own church's emphasis? How might Jesus' call to "go" into the world (Figure 3) be strengthened in your church?
3. In Chapter 3, five characteristics of ministry were outlined (p.45–49). What are the distinctive contributions of your church, or family of churches? What are the opportunities and challenges of those characteristics? How might you share your church's strengths for the benefit of others?

Recommended Books on Culture.

1. Andy Crouch, *Culture Making: Recovering Our Creative Calling* (Downers Grove, IL: InterVarsity Press, 2008). A helpful integration of cultural questions in the light of the gospel and a Christian's calling.
2. T. Desmond Alexander, *From Eden to the New Jerusalem: Exploring God's Plan for Life on Earth*, (Nottingham, UK: IVP, 2008). The purpose of God for the world, revealed through focussing on the presence of God, from Genesis to Revelation.
3. Philip Jenkins, *The Next Christendom: The Coming of Global*

Christianity (Oxford University Press, 2002). A stimulating view of Christianity, with its new emphases, as seen across the world.

PART TWO

THEOLOGY

CHAPTER 4

God's Transformation of People

In Part One we have taken a brief look at the world and its cultures in which we have been called to live and serve. It is a diverse mix of deeply challenging features, but it is also brimming with opportunities for the power of the gospel. Part Two moves on to consider some of the theological foundations that we need in order to respond with good biblical practices (discussed in Part Three). For Christians to make a difference in the world, we must be clear about God's purposes.

Asking the Right Questions

Virtually every social commentator would agree that the Western world is currently living between paradigms. It is a period of dramatic change in which the fixed and familiar markers in society are moving. Rushing, however, to the practical "how" questions relating to our church practices (Part Three) will cause us to rely on methods lifted from the past or to grab at every new idea.

God's Transformation of People

What we need, especially in times of great change, is to base our practices on solid theological ground. These are the "who" and "what" questions. The person of Jesus stands at the centre. Christ shapes everything. He, therefore, is the place to start: who he is, and what he has done (Christology). It is noteworthy that at the time of the Reformation the far-reaching changes and renewal that came to the church were based upon deep theological convictions. It is by looking at Christ that we see what God's purpose is for the world (missiology), and from that standpoint, we are able to shape the church to join his purposes (ecclesiology). So – Christ, then mission, then church. Christology leads to missiology; missiology leads to ecclesiology.

Historically, the church has often reversed this sequence. When the primary questions revolve around the church (its structures and programmes), it runs the risk of becoming detached from its true vocation of glorifying Christ and showing him to the world. Our thinking must move forward in the particular sequence: Christology informs missiology, which in turn determines our ecclesiology. This is represented by Figure 4.[53]

---

[53] I am indebted to Alan Hirsch for the basis of this diagram and the thinking that lies behind it. Hirsch, *The Forgotten Ways,* 142f.

Figure 4. Asking the Right Questions

WHO?		WHAT?		HOW?
Christology	Determines →	**Missiology**	Determines →	**Ecclesiology**
The Person and Work of Jesus		The Purpose of God and His People		The Form and Function of the Church

The above three questions are the theological building blocks for God's transformation of people (Chapter 4); God's mission in his world (Chapter 5); and God's activity through his church (Chapter 6).

The Urgent Need for Christian Transformation

What exactly are we called to do in the world and its culture? Are we called to transform and change it? Is that our role? Is it even possible? Culture is the scene of man's rebellion and judgement and also the setting of God's mercy. The biblical story, indeed culture's story, tells us that there will not be a dead-end but ultimately a new beginning. Transformation and making something new is at the heart of God's intention in the world.

It is precisely at this point that Andy Crouch in his book, *Culture Making: Recovering Our Creative Calling,* argues that we are confronted with a paradox.[54] Changing the world is the one thing we seem incapable of doing. Grand sounding Christian slogans are everywhere, "Let's change the world". This sounds extremely impressive until we consider how poorly we do at even changing our own little lives. We talk about engaging and

---

[54]Crouch, *Culture Making.*

transforming the culture, when in fact it tends to transform us.

Richard Foster writes in the Foreword of *The Spirit of the Disciplines*, "Nothing is more apparent today than our inability to live as we know we should".[55] Political, social and self-help recipes seek to liberate mankind's bondage. However, societies the world around, are currently in desperate straits trying to produce people who are barely capable of coping with their life on earth in a non-destructive manner. Against this background, only a few voices have continued to emphasise a spiritual solution. They point out that social and political initiatives have shown no tendency to transform the heart. There is a growing epidemic of depression, suicide, personal emptiness, and escapism.

If the cure is spiritual, how does Christianity fit into the answer? In another of his books, *Renovation of the Heart*, Dallas Willard asserts that Christianity has largely been failing: "Christianity has not been imparting effectual answers to the vital questions of human existence. At least, not to wide ranges of self-identifying Christians, and obviously not to non-Christians".[56] True conversion to Christ has nothing to do with becoming a Christianized version of what we already are. That is a rejection of God's salvation and will not bring about the necessary change and transformation.

What newness is required?

We noted in Chapter 3 that a great many "new" initiatives, programmes and church structures have been tried. But do we

---

[55] Dallas Willard, *The Spirit of the Disciplines: Understanding How God Changes Lives* (London: Hodder and Stoughton, 1996), ix.
[56] Dallas Willard, *Renovation of the Heart: Putting on the Character of Christ* (Colorado Springs, CO: Navpress, 2002), 21.

lose sight of the essential point? The Bible clearly speaks about "newness". In fact it is replete with this language – new song, new thing, new covenant, new mercies, new heart and spirit, new wine, new tongues, new command, new life, new creation, new birth, new name, new heaven and earth – to mention but some of the phrases. Without exception, the newness that is referred to is what God, not man, initiates and accomplishes. Looking a little closer we see that, for example, "a new song" invariably has content that is old! It always has to do with God's rescue and salvation. So the Psalmist writes, "Sing to the Lord a new song; ... sing to the Lord, praise His name; proclaim his *salvation* day after day" (Psalm 96:1,2) and "Sing to the Lord a new song, for he has done marvellous things; his right hand and his holy arm have worked *salvation* for him" (Psalm 98:1).

Churches can exhaust themselves by fixating on structural issues and programmes when the life and need is elsewhere. This is the point made by Colin Marshall and Tony Payne in their book, *The Trellis and The Vine*.[57] They argue that ministry should focus more attention on the vine (representing the central disciple-making work of Christian ministry) and less on the trellis (representing the structure and support for ministry). It is a point well made – gospel growth is primary and requires greater attention than church growth. Or to express it theologically, Christology is the source of life and purpose for both missiology and ecclesiology.

---

[57] Colin Marshall and Tony Payne, *The Trellis And The Vine: The Ministry Mind-Shift That Changes Everything* (Sydney, Australia: Matthias Media, 2009).

Nominalism and the Human Heart

The Bible bears testimony to a waywardness in the human heart and a Christian nominalism poorly disguised under a religious veneer. In the Old Testament, faithlessness is a chronic problem, exemplified in Israel's wilderness experience. Israel came to live as a theocracy, with religious requirements codified as an essential aspect of national law, much as is the case in Islamic nations today. However, despite constant warnings against disobedience to God's commands, Israel persistently distanced herself from God and his ways. Law does not change the heart. Yet the Law remains and is necessary. But it is striking that Jesus, in expounding the Law in the Sermon on the Mount, begins with eight Beatitudes or blessings. Jesus introduces what is new by starting with blessing rather than judgement.

The period covered by the four gospels recounts the presence of God's kingdom in powerful ways. Yet Jesus makes it clear that even the frequent occurrence of miracles are not, of themselves, sufficient to safeguard against complacency or outright rejection of his message (Matthew 11:20–24). Furthermore, Jesus experienced many disciples who turned back and no longer followed him (John 6:66), and even the twelve underwent a crisis of faith and deserted him at the crucial moment (Matthew 26:31).

The New Testament letters testify to churches of that age having as many problems as churches today. Among the challenges for Paul and his colleagues were: how to counter the constant erosion of God's good news (Galatians 1:6–7); growth in Christ-like character (1 Thessalonians 4:3–8); dealing with divisiveness (1 Corinthians 3:1–17); loss of first love (Philippians 2:21); and outright apostasy (Hebrews 3:12–19). Eddie

Gibbs, in his study on modern day nominalism, concludes that spiritual atrophy is influenced by "inconsistencies in the church ... the pressures of society as well as through the individual's spiritual life".[58]

The Kingdom of God's Transforming Vision

A revolution that works

In the Sermon on the Mount, Jesus paints such a bold picture of kingdom life that many question whether it is at all possible. A kingdom where a lustful look amounts to adultery and anger against a brother is like murder! But Jesus is not theorising about moral evil and personal goodness. He is deliberately taking a concrete (and seemingly shocking) approach because he is bringing something altogether new. It is disastrous to think that he is giving more "laws" – laws that we will find impossible to keep. Rather, Jesus is fulfilling what the prophets foretold, that God would write his law on our hearts (Jeremiah 31:33). He would change our inner self.

Jesus illustrates this by painting the picture of a fruit tree bearing good fruit because of its inner nature. In fact he goes further and says, "A good tree cannot bear bad fruit" (Matthew 7:18). God's transformation changes the whole "tree". It is not behaviour modification; it is the gift of a new heart. This "goodness" speaks of followers of Jesus engaging with his life to such an extent that their goal is to become people for whom sin is not even interesting. This is nothing short of a revolution for humankind. The life of the kingdom of heaven is now one of

---

[58]Eddie Gibbs, *In Name Only: Tackling the Problem of Nominal Christianity* (Pasadena, CA: Fuller Seminary Press, 1994), 70.

our options. Jesus illustrates in his teaching how those alive in the kingdom can now live. Transformation works as a gift from the inside out. As he said, "The kingdom of God is within you" (Luke 17:21).

Richard Rohr takes us to the heart of the matter. He points out that "Transformation ... is not the same as change."[59] Change is when something new begins. Transformation tends to be just the opposite. It happens after a crisis, when something old is taken away. Of course, not all crises lead to transformation, but the loss associated with a crisis is fertile ground for God's purposes. The transformation of which Jesus speaks involves an encounter, a confrontation with God's King. The old has to give way for the new to come. God is intent on making new people for a new kingdom.

Deeply imbedded in the New Testament, and found at the heart of the Lord's Prayer, is the belief and hope that God's kingdom will come and his will will be done, on earth as it is in heaven. However, the kingdom of heaven is not a location, it is a *fact* – God is ruling. In Jesus, believers have a new accessibility to the rule of the heavens. What is at hand? The kingdom that was in Jesus. As people looked at him and listened to him, they realised God's longed-for kingdom was present, and that its life was being offered to them now. Others are to look at followers of Jesus, see this life of God and his kingdom and say, "This is the best thing I have ever seen. I must have it."

This is the context within which we understand the Sermon on the Mount. Willard comments, "The brilliance and profundity of Jesus stand out ... as he forcefully conveys an under-

---

[59]Richard Rohr, *Jesus' Plan for a New World: The Sermon on the Mount* (Cincinnati, OH: St. Anthony Messenger Press, 1996), 120.

standing of human life that actually works."[60] Further, the Sermon deeply undermines Israel's nationalistic agenda for a kingdom. Jesus was totally opposed to such an agenda because, as N.T. Wright explains, "He saw it as, paradoxically, a way of being deeply disloyal to Israel's God, and to his purposes for Israel to be the Light of the World."[61] Jesus' communication of God's kingdom continually indicates that it, quite simply and powerfully, is the sphere of God's effective will and the "place" in which transformation becomes possible.

The King of the kingdom

The good news of the kingdom of God found in the gospels is the foundation upon which God's new community, made up of new people, is built. The depth and extent of this gospel foundation can only be grasped by seeing who Jesus is and embracing the entirety of his mission. Jesus is the Son of God (Mark 1:1), God's only King (John 18:37). His kingdom proclamation, teaching and demonstration, his atoning death, transforming resurrection and promise of the Spirit, together with his ascension and glorious return are all essential to the kingdom message.

The good news which Jesus proclaimed, is that the life of God's kingdom is now available. We experience this new life by placing our confidence fully in Jesus for everything. The gospel of the kingdom invites us to become a different kind of person – a transformed person – not just a person who is trying to live in a different way. It is a gift, God's grace at work, bringing

---

[60]Dallas Willard, *The Divine Conspiracy: Rediscovering Our Hidden Life in God* (London: Fount Paperbacks, Harper Collins Publishers, 1998), 152.
[61]N.T. Wright, *The Challenge of Jesus* (London: SPCK, 2000), 26.

about what we cannot accomplish on our own.

The reason Jesus' message and agenda continued to be taken seriously after his death, was because the first followers so deeply believed God had raised him from the dead. Not that he had gone to heaven leaving his body behind somewhere, but that he had somehow gone right through death and into a new form of physicality. The early Christians were as puzzled by this as we are, but clung on to the truth that God would raise the dead to new life. "They were not ready for a dramatic action whereby one man would be raised from the dead ahead of time, bringing to birth a whole new mode of being yet to be completed. But that, they believed emphatically and unanimously, was what had happened".[62] It is the culminating death and resurrection of Jesus the King that achieves and validates God's kingdom transformation, whereby an individual become its citizen.

Some kingdom realities about transformation

Different statements about the kingdom are found in the gospels. For example, we read: that the kingdom of God is coming immediately, "The time has come … the kingdom of God is near" (Mark 1:15); has already arrived in Jesus, "But if I drive out demons by the finger of God, then the kingdom of God has come to you" (Luke 11:20); has been delayed – the five foolish virgins were unprepared because the bridegroom was "a long time in coming" (Matthew 25:5); and it will appear some time in the future, "he went on to tell them a parable because he was near Jerusalem and the people thought that the kingdom of God was going to appear at once" (Luke 19:11).

---

[62] Tom Wright, *The Myth of the Millennium* (London: Azure, 1999), 76.

This "already but not yet" dimension of the kingdom creates a dynamic tension for our spiritual transformation. Rohr describes this as living in "a threshold space between this world and the next. You learn how to live between heaven and earth one foot in both worlds ... It will be a collision of opposites."[63] Jesus' proclamation led the early Christians to believe that they were living not so much in the last days (though that was true) as in the first days of God's *new* creation.

It would be wrong to put all the eschatological weight on that which is still to come. The testimony of New Testament Christianity is that in Jesus, the "end" has come forward into the present. There is, of course, a danger in distorting the picture in one direction or the other. It is possible to so emphasise the discontinuity between the present world and the future world that we are left indifferent to seeing the world change. On the other hand, it is possible to so emphasise the continuity between the present world and the coming new world, that some have imagined the kingdom of God is being built on earth through their own hard work. Bodily resurrection surely indicates a vital continuity as well as a radical discontinuity between this world and the next, what is and what is to come. The new world has already begun with Easter and Pentecost.

The fact that believers live within this framework enables us to come to terms with our varied experiences of progress as well as failure, joy and struggle. Set in this kingdom context, spiritual transformation has the clear understanding of justification, sanctification, and glorification. On the one hand, as John writes, "No one who lives in him keeps on sinning" (1 John 3:6). On the other hand, "If we claim to be without sin, we deceive ourselves and the truth is not in us" (1 John 1:8).

---

[63]Rohr, *Jesus' Plan for a New World*, 111.

Knowing that there is a coming day when everything, including us, will be perfected, God's people can be emboldened to press in to all the goodness and power found in the presence of the kingdom.

Judgement and the completion of the kingdom's transformation

In kingdom writing today, we hear much about the new heavens and earth, which God has promised. This is a welcome and necessary emphasis because it lifts our eyes to God's ultimate and glorious purpose for this world. However, we hear very little of the eschatological reality of God's judgement. "The present heavens and earth are reserved for fire, being kept for the day of judgement and the destruction of ungodly men" (2 Timothy 3:7 cf. Hebrews 9:27–28). Time and again it seems to be airbrushed out of the end-time scenario.

Judgement, however, is an essential ingredient for the future creation of the new heavens and a new earth. By it, God purifies and removes the presence of all evil "so that the righteous will shine like the sun" (Matthew 13:41–43). This is necessary for a new world.

Judgement is simply a matter of declaring the truth. It gets past our rationalisations and explanations, and we will look in that Day and say, "That is true. That's what I was. That's what I did." This does not, however, bring into question a disciple's salvation. We do not have something to "pay" in the future at the Day of Judgement. That would contradict and deny the good news. Some people seem to think that God is only interested in marking down the bad things and keeping score. That is a terrible view of God. God deeply cares about who we become.

This vision of final judgement, Peter reminds us, is given to stimulate our holiness, love and witness: "Since everything will be destroyed in this way, what kind of people ought you to be? You ought to live holy and godly lives as you look forward to the day of God and speed its coming" (2 Peter 3:11–12).

Judgement keeps us in touch with the awfulness of human lostness. It was people's rejection of God and the inevitability of judgement that led to Jesus' grief and weeping over the city of Jerusalem (Luke 19:41–44). In the same way, Paul wrote of his "great sorrow and unceasing anguish" for his own race. His heart's desire and prayer to God was for their salvation (Romans 9:1–3, 10:1). Ignoring judgement diminishes the gravity of sin and the unsurpassed love and grace of the cross. This the Bible refuses to do because release from just judgement is profound good news.

The Ingredients for Christian Transformation

John Stott, in his last sermon after a long life of Christian ministry, reflection and writing, expressed where his mind had come to rest on what was most important. A hush fell on the gathered assembly and he said simple words to the effect that God wants his people to become like Christ. Christ-likeness – followers of Jesus learning to become like Jesus.

Nothing short of spiritual rebirth can initiate this new life (John 3:3), which God then continues to purify. "Being transformed into his likeness with ever-increasing glory, which comes from the Lord who is the Spirit" (2 Corinthians 3:18, 5:15). This process of transformation, however, is far from quick or easy. A deep application of the gospel of grace, co-operation with the Holy Spirit together with the use of spiritual disciplines moves us forward in transformation.

The Gospel of Grace and Transformation

Gospel confusions

A number of confusions arise about the message of the gospel itself when it comes to transformation. The first mistake is to think that the gospel is only for unbelievers, and is limited to their initiation into the Christian faith. This is to confuse the starting line with the finishing line. In fact, the gospel continues to be crucial for a disciple's development, and the way in turns out to be also the way on. The second issue is even more fundamental. What gospel is being proclaimed, and is that gospel actually Jesus' gospel? The answer to this question has huge bearing on the sorts of disciples that are made.

Willard contends that some contemporary "gospels" seem to focus on what he calls "sin management".[64] These speak of guaranteeing one's place in heaven, and of correcting some moral and social behaviour. These are both, obviously, matters of great importance, but they say little, or nothing, about the transforming power of Jesus now. "Lostness" is not just something people will experience if they die without Christ; rather, all of us are already "lost" here on earth, and that reality reflects itself in our inability to live life as God intended. His salvation begins now.

Gospel debate

The nature of the gospel, what it is and what it does, will be a critical issue in every generation. The debate, both in the Christian church and in the secular world in recent years, has had a familiar ring. The liberal view insists that Paul's gospel of

---

[64] Willard, *The Divine Conspiracy*, 43f.

justification is sharply different from Jesus' gospel of the kingdom. This idea is widespread: that Paul "messed up" what Jesus had initiated. Nor is it just proposed in Christian circles. It is seen in secular writers, such as Philip Pullman, in his book, *The Good Man Jesus and the Scoundrel Christ*. Here he says the "good human" Jesus is distorted into a divine saviour figure by people like Paul. Modern Muslim apologists have argued a similar case. They are happy with the prophet Jesus but not the divine Son of God. This perceived variance, between Jesus in the gospels and Paul in the epistles, is false.

This criticism, however, highlights our need to understand the *unity* of the New Testament. "Kingdom" terminology is biblical language and therefore conveys something important. We need both the language of the gospels as well as that of the epistles. Jesus powerfully linked his kingdom message with the necessity of atonement. All the four gospels have the cross and resurrection as the culmination of Jesus' mission. Jesus' atoning death as the Son of God is there in the Last Supper, with its Passover associations of the sacrificial lamb. The aim is to hold together, in the one gospel, the truth and insights contained in the whole of the New Testament. The overarching kingdom message is deeply embedded in substitutionary atonement. Without God's atoning grace, the message of the kingdom can communicate a weak view of sin (and inevitably offering a weak cure) with a potentially legalistic message to join Jesus' "kingdom programme". And without the kingdom, the doctrines of justification and atonement can push some aspects God's present reality into the future and produce a narrow individualism with limited concern for God's whole world.

Gospel salvation

The gospel of grace speaks about salvation. The salvation Christ gives to his people is freedom from sin in all its ugly manifestations, liberation into a new life and finally attaining "the glorious liberty of the children of God". We have been saved, we are being saved, and we will be saved.

The past phase of salvation (justification) is the reality that we have been set free from inevitable judgement. John Stott comments on the logical sequence of thought in Romans 1:16–18 which links the power of God, the righteousness of God and the wrath of God. He writes, "It is because his wrath is revealed against sin that his righteousness is revealed in the gospel and his power through the gospel to believers".[65]

The present phase of salvation (sanctification) recognises that sin is still active in the believer. Salvation is also a present work in progress. It is deliverance from the bondage of self-centredness into a growing Christ-likeness. Therefore Paul exhorts the Philippians, "Continue to work out your salvation with fear and trembling for it is God who works in you" (Philippians 2:12,13), and Peter stresses the need for his readers to "Grow up in your salvation" (1 Peter 2:2). Luther described fallen man as curved inwards upon himself. It is from this prison of self that Christ liberates us through sanctification.

The future state of salvation (glorification) recognises that each day brings us closer to that goal, "Our salvation is nearer now than when we first believed" (Romans 13:11). This will include the redemption of our bodies (Romans 8:23), with all transformation complete in a flash, in the twinkling of an eye

---

[65]John Stott, *Christian Mission in the Modern World*, (Coventry, UK: Falcon, CPAS, 1975), 103.

(1 Corinthians 15:51–52).

Any failure to embrace this integrated theology of salvation will lead to an under-emphasis of the regeneration and transformation of the believer. Regeneration stresses the inception of a new state of being in contrast with the old. The Spirit continues the work of transformation. The two operating powers that produce this new life are described in Titus 3:5 as "the washing of rebirth and renewal by the Holy Spirit".

The Spirit and Regeneration

The church of today does not always live the life of the Spirit as outlined in the New Testament. Gordon Fee argues that the "evidential dimension of life in the Spirit, probably more than anything else, separates believers in later church history from those in Paul's churches."[66] The marginalising of the Spirit in some quarters of scholarship, and the frequent domestication of the Spirit by the church, have surely made us poorer.

Dependence on the power of the Spirit is a much-needed emphasis in a world that believes human activity can accomplish anything. Only the Holy Spirit can open eyes, enlighten darkness and liberate a person from bondage. Certainly repentance and faith are to be our response (Acts 2:38) but even they are clearly seen as gifts of God (Ephesians 2:8).

The Spirit and Christian initiation

The Spirit is crucial at the entry point of conversion. In fact the Spirit is the identity marker of the converted. In Galatians 3:1–5 Paul appeals to the experienced reality of the Spirit by

---

[66] Gordon Fee, *Paul, the Spirit and the People of God* (London: Hodder and Stoughton, 1997), 143.

which the Galatian believers started their path of Christian discipleship. The one question he asks about their initiation as Christians is, "Did you receive the Spirit by observing the law or by believing?" (Galatians 3:2) Knowing that they had received the Spirit seems to have been an unmistakeable experience. However, as Fee explains, "When we receive the Spirit at conversion divine perfection does not set in, but divine 'infection' does. We have been invaded by the living God himself, in the person of the Spirit, whose goal is to infect us thoroughly with God's own likeness."[67]

In 2 Thessalonians 2:13, Paul refers to their experience of salvation as being brought about "through the sanctifying work of the Spirit and through belief in the truth." Salvation, for Paul, has to do with both entry and participation in God's salvation. It means to be joined to the people of God by the Spirit, and to live the life of a saved person.

The Spirit and sanctification

In the third book of his *Institutes*, John Calvin deals with his subjects in a fascinating order. He writes about faith and regeneration, penitence and the life of a Christian person. It is only then that he comes to deal with justification. Perhaps by beginning with regeneration and the Christian life, Calvin may have wished to emphasise that justification by faith was in no way a pretext for a passive attitude towards discipleship. The question that Calvin asks is: How can we appropriate Christ's salvation, and receive the grace that accomplishes it? He writes, "We now have to see how the blessings that God the Father has committed to his Son are to reach us, seeing that the Son did not

---

[67]Ibid., 111.

receive them for his own use, but to bring them to the poor and needy."[68] He sees regeneration as the outcome of justification by faith. Once again, we see that the need theologically is to take hold of sanctification as firmly as we do justification and glorification.

A genuine recapturing of Paul's perspective will not isolate the Spirit, nor exalt the Spirit. Rather, it will cause the church to be more vitally Trinitarian. Salvation is God's activity from beginning to end. The Father initiated it, in that it belongs to God's eternal purposes (1 Corinthians 2:6–9), and it has God as its ultimate goal (1 Corinthians 8:6). Christ the Son accomplishes salvation through his death and resurrection, and is the central feature of all of Paul's theology. Transforming sanctification is the work of the Spirit, growing Christ-like fruit in our lives.

Sanctifying grace

Effective discipleship needs the ongoing explanation and application of the gospel, and this is succinctly expressed by Richard Lovelace. Many Christians, he writes, "rely on their sanctification for their justification" even though they know doctrinally it is the other way around.[69] Our tendency in every day life is to draw our sense of assurance and spiritual well-being from our recent religious performance, such as a good quiet time or a reasonably pure thought life. But this in effect drives us away

---

[68]John Calvin, *Institutes of the Christian Religion: Book Third* (London: James Clarke and Co. Ltd., 1949, Chapter 1), 462.

[69]Richard F. Lovelace writes about this confusion in *Dynamics of Spiritual Life: An Evangelical Theology of Renewal*, (Downers Grove, IL: IVP Academic, 1979), 101; as does Martin Lloyd-Jones in *Spiritual Depression: Its Causes and Cures,* (London: Marshall Pickering, 1998), Chapter 2, The True Foundation.

from the gospel of grace and back to religion: "I live a reasonably good life and therefore God accepts me" rather than "I am accepted through Jesus, and therefore I want to please him".

The human heart persistently defaults to religion, wishing to believe that our performance makes us acceptable to God. The good news proclaims the opposite: God's acceptance and forgiveness has nothing to do with either our goodness or badness. It solely rests on *his* goodness and *his* performance. This is expressed by Jesus, no more simply than in his parable of the pharisee and the tax collector (Luke 18:9–14). The pharisee boasted he was good enough ("confident in his own righteousness") while the tax collector knew that he wasn't saying, "God, have mercy on me a sinner". Only he (the tax collector) went home "justified".

Spiritual Disciplines and Character Formation

A means of grace

Spiritual disciplines, utilised by Christians down through the centuries, are only an extension, not always wisely done, of practices followed by Jesus and his earliest friends. Solitude, prayer, service, study and much more are all there. Paul also recognizes the need for such practices and therefore writes to Timothy exhorting him, "Train yourself to be godly. For physical training is of some value, but godliness has value for all things holding promise for both the present life and the life to come" (1 Timothy 4:7,8).

But let's be clear. The path of practising spiritual disciplines does not in itself produce transformation. Rather it puts us in a place where change can occur. The disciplines allow us to be before God so that he can transform us. It is not us, but

God. The disciplines lead us to him who is "Spirit and life" (John 6:63). By doing what we *can* do (spiritual disciplines), we receive from God the resources to do what we *cannot* do (live an increasingly transformed life).

A fear associated with spiritual disciplines is that we may degenerate into legalism. This, however, is not the major problem facing Western Christianity, nor should it be an excuse for weak discipleship. Believers grow in Christ-likeness by well-directed effort. Grace is not opposed to effort, but it is opposed to earning. Nothing of salvation or transformation is earned. People are saved by grace but are not to be paralysed by grace. In fact an ancient dictum expressed it this way: "The saint consumes more grace than the sinner."[70] This is because everything the saint does in living Christ's life requires, and is done through, grace. James writes about followers of Jesus having "more grace" (James 4:6). Paul makes it clear that God causes grace to abound for "every good work" (2 Corinthians 9:8). The purpose, therefore, of spiritual disciplines is to connect us more firmly with God's grace through Jesus and his Spirit.

Learning from others

Church history provides a rich and thought-provoking story of spiritual disciplines. The Desert Fathers of the fourth century believed that a radical response, with decisive action, was the only way to experience deep salvation. They saw that the pagan society in which they lived, together with its values, needed to be challenged rather than passively accepted. For the Desert Fathers a life of solitude provided that challenge. Solitude was not a private, therapeutic escape, but a place of conversion. In

[70] Dallas Willard, Class Lecture from "Spirituality and Ministry," Fuller Theological Seminary, June 7–18, 2004.

The Way of the Heart, Henri Nouwen writes that, "Solitude is the place of the great struggle and the great encounter."[71] Solitude can have the effect of removing the scaffolding from our life in order to face our compulsions.

These followers of Jesus were committed to getting a foothold on solid ground so that real change could be experienced. Clearly the present world is different from theirs, and believers today must discover God's way of liberation in their context. As Thomas Merton explains, "We cannot do exactly what they did. But we must be as thorough and as ruthless in our determination to break all spiritual chains and ... to discover and develop our inalienable spiritual liberty."[72]

The disciplines are about coming to know, and experiencing in a deeper way, the unconditional love and forgiveness of God. In that place we see our own need and sinfulness more clearly and recognize that God's grace, released through these disciplines, assists us in putting off the old and putting on the new.

The ordinary events of life

The circumstances of life are the arena of God's activity. If we discard each opportunity for growth as not being "right", we end up with no place to receive God's kingdom into our lives. It is precisely through the ordinary events of life, work, and relationships that believers are positioned to grow in sanctification, with the assistance of spiritual disciplines. Scripture provides no universal way of proceeding on this path. Each of us will need to develop our own list of spiritual disciplines.

---

[71] Henri J.M. Nouwen, *The Way of the Heart: Desert Spirituality and Contemporary Ministry* (San Francisco: Harper Collins, 1991), 26.
[72] Thomas Merton, *The Wisdom of the Desert* (New York: New Directions Publishing, 1970), 24.

The disciplines of abstinence, such as fasting and solitude, are to be counter-balanced and supplemented by disciplines of engagement, such as the use of Scripture and service. Rather than attempting to compile a complete list of spiritual practices, we are encouraged to find those disciplines which particularly touch an area of life in need of transformation. If, for example, we enjoy time alone with God and finds that replenishing, we will also need disciplines that lead us consistently into community and fellowship; while those who love being with people, and are energised by that, will benefit from strengthening the discipline of time alone with God.

Jesus, who he is and what he did, sent by the Father and empowered by the Holy Spirit, is unique in giving us the only way to personal transformation. Christ living in us, the hope of glory.

We now move from the basis of our transformation (Christology) to God's purpose in the world (missiology).

CHAPTER FIVE

God's Mission in His World

Followers of Jesus everywhere must think, at some time or other, about their purpose and the purpose of the church in the world. What should our relationship be to the world? What is our role and responsibility? In reply to these questions most Christians would make some use of the term "mission". However, there is a wide divergence in understanding what "mission" means. We might say, "Well, theology is all about God (the study of God) and mission is what we get to do (our part)". Mission is often thought about in relation to human endeavours and projects of various kinds. But is this correct? Is this what the Bible says?

The Missional Basis of the Bible

Mission is what the story of the Bible is all about. It is the Bible's "grand narrative", its overarching story: God's rescue for the whole world. "The whole Bible is itself a missional phenomenon", so writes Christopher Wright in his fine book, *The*

Mission of God.[73] He tells the story of finding himself teaching a module called, "The Biblical Basis of Mission" and coming to the conclusion that the course needed to be renamed, "The Missional Basis of the Bible".

Mission is God's from start to finish. "It is not the church that has a mission of salvation to fulfill in the world; it is the mission of the Son and the Spirit through the Father that includes the church".[74] David Bosch underlines this perspective further by distinguishing between "mission", singular, which is primary, and "missions" in the plural, being a derivative.[75] Whatever mission activities we ourselves may engage in, they are only authentic in so far as they participate in the mission of God.

Towards a definition of mission

"Mission means our committed participation as God's people, at God's invitation and command, in God's own mission within the history of God's world for the redemption of God's creation."[76]

This definition offered by Wright presents the expanse of God's mission. Scripture straddles God's vast purposes for the creation whilst never allowing us to lose sight of his personal concern and rescue for individuals (Colossians 3:1–4). God's

---

[73]Christopher J.H. Wright, *The Mission of God: Unlocking the Bible's Grand Narrative* (Nottingham, UK: Inter-Varsity Press, 2006), 22.

[74]Jürgen Moltmann, *The Church in the Power of the Spirit: A Contribution to Messianic Ecclesiology* (Minneapolis, MN: Augsburg Fortress, 1993).

[75]David J. Bosch, *Transforming Mission: Paradigm Shifts in Theology of Mission* (Maryknoll, NY: Orbis Books, 2007), 391.

[76]Wright, *The Mission of God*, 22–23f.

mission embraces the temporal and eternal, the present and the future, the personal and the global. God the Father lovingly initiated it (John 3:16), God the Son sacrificially atoned for it (1 Peter 3:18), God the Spirit powerfully confirms it (Romans 8:22–23). Throughout this book I use the word "missional", such as *missional* church or *missional* leadership, to describe a commitment to God's purpose to redeem the world.

We know that the Bible ends with a vision of the new heavens and earth. This is where God's mission is majestically headed. Foreseen prophetically in the Old Testament, Isaiah pictures a world where wolf and lamb lie down together and where peace, justice and righteousness "forevermore" are seen (Isaiah 9:7, 11:6). In the final chapters of Isaiah, the language has become explicit: "Behold I will create new heavens and a new earth. The former things will not be remembered, nor will they come to mind" (Isaiah 65:17). In the New Testament Paul writes that the whole creation "waits" for its liberation from decay, as do believers (Romans 8:19–25). "They (the early Christians) believed that God was going to do for the whole cosmos what he had done for Jesus at Easter."[77]

The scope of God's mission

Creation and redemption are the purposeful actions of God's mission. Three features are noteworthy.

First, the earth and all creation belong to God (Psalm 24:1, Colossians 1:15–20). Man's mandate is to steward the earth. In fact, this is our first "great commission" (Genesis 1:28, 2:15). Care of the creation is not an *ecocentric* view of the world, elevating the creation above God and his stewards. Rather, it is an

---

[77]Tom Wright, *Surprised by Hope* (London: SPCK, 2007), 104.

unselfish act of love and obedience, done for the sake of future generations and in defence of the poor and powerless of the earth, for the glory of God.

Secondly, the extent and impact of sin mark out the breadth of God's mission. The Fall has affected every dimension of the creation – the physical, spiritual, rational and social (Genesis 3, Romans 1,2). Sin affects human society and history. "Sin spreads horizontally within society and sin propagates itself vertically between generations."[78]

Thirdly, God's mission strives for social justice. This was a primary concern of the Old Testament prophetic tradition (e.g. Micah 6:8). While the socio-political context of the early church was fundamentally different, it would be simplistic and wrong to conclude that the New Testament had become more "spiritual" and less concerned with justice (e.g. Acts 6:1–4).

The biblical witness to the scope of God's mission is seen to be profoundly *theocentric*. It puts both humanity and the rest of creation within the orbit of God's wider redemptive purposes and plans.

What We Believe About Jesus and His Mission

The central message is that God is reclaiming the whole world as his own, in and through Jesus. Far from being the imposition of a dehumanising tyranny, God's kingdom comes to confront the tyrannies which plague this world – greed, poverty, war, disease, and death. Jesus comes to restore genuine humanness, justice, and salvation. What we believe, teach and practise about these things is of vital importance. Dr. Derek Morphew's book, *Breakthrough,* provides an outstanding introduction and

---

[78]Wright, *The Mission of God*, 431.

teaching on the significance of the kingdom of God.[79]

Biblical doctrine – A Vineyard expression

The proper role and use of doctrine is to provide open, clear teaching, with the aim that disciples of Jesus come to understand him and the things of God better. A problem arises when doctrine is taught in a way that says you must believe this, no matter what you think or believe. That doesn't work well. Jesus, not our doctrine, is the truth, and the Holy Spirit is the Spirit of truth. As Jesus said, it is as a disciple holds to *his* teaching that truth is known, a truth which sets us free (John 8:31–32).

C.S. Lewis famously argued that the best remedy against theological error is to have a plain, basic, Christian orthodoxy, shorn of denominational agendas. This is what he meant by "mere Christianity", a phrase he came across in the writings of Richard Baxter (1615–1691). The main and the plain is what we need, and we are all the richer for those who have sought to express this for us. I am thankful for those in my own church movement who have contributed to our doctrinal understanding, and I offer some reflections on this.

The theological approach expressed in the Vineyard Statement of Faith aligns itself with both the centrality and entirety of Jesus' kingdom mission. Post-modernism may assert that there was, and is, no universal story, no meta-narrative which offers a comprehensive picture of reality. The Statement refutes that view by offering not only a clear theological structure, but also God's biblical story of redemptive history.[80] As Dr. Don

---

[79] Dr. Derek Morphew, *Breakthrough: Discovering the Kingdom* (Cape Town: Vineyard International Publishing, 2007).
[80] See Vineyard Statement of Faith in Appendix 3, in Jackson, *The Quest For the Radical Middle*, 397–401.

Williams, one of the principal architects of the Statement, comments, "Perhaps anticipating post-modernism's stress on stories we too have a story to tell. It is the story of the kingdom."[81] Rather than simply reproducing a Trinitarian structure (as in the Apostles' Creed), the Statement narrates the mission of God, as King. In the Apostles' Creed, Jesus is confessed as God's Son, "conceived by the Holy Ghost, born of the Virgin Mary, suffered under Pontius Pilate, was crucified".

By contrast the Statement not only speaks of Jesus' incarnation and atonement, but also of the kingdom ministry accomplished through His life: "Jesus was anointed as God's Messiah and empowered by the Holy Spirit, inaugurating God's kingdom reign on earth, overpowering the reign of Satan by resisting temptation, preaching the good news of salvation, healing the sick, casting out demons and raising the dead. Gathering his disciples, He reconstituted God's people as his church to be the instrument of his kingdom."[82] This is the basis of our mission.

The structuring of this Statement may lead some to believe that there has been a dilution of atonement theology in favour of kingdom theology. This however cannot be an either/or issue but rather a question of full inclusion and balance. Wright expands the point in his book, *Surprised by Hope,* "We [have to] reintegrate what should never have been separated – the kingdom-inaugurating public work of Jesus on the one hand

---

[81] Don Williams, "Why Vineyard: A Theological Reflection." KingdomRain.net.
http://www.kingdomrain.net/index.php?option=com_content&task=view&id=212&Itemid=33 (accessed July 19th 2008).
[82] Jackson, *The Quest for the Radical Middle,* 399.

and his redemptive death and resurrection on the other."[83] Calvary is the centre of God's redeeming mission. It is the wonder into which eternity will gaze. The atonement is central and crucial, and the Vineyard's Statement reveals Jesus' ministry culminating in his death and resurrection. The meaning of his death is expressed classically: "in his sinless, perfect life Jesus met the demands of the law and in his atoning death on the cross he took God's judgement for sin which we deserve as lawbreakers. By his death on the cross he also disarmed the demonic powers."[84]

The Statement goes on to speak of the outpouring of the Spirit on the Day of Pentecost. "The Spirit brings the permanent indwelling presence of God to us for spiritual worship, personal sanctification, building up the church, gifting us for ministry, and driving back the kingdom of Satan by the evangelisation of the world through proclaiming the word of Jesus and doing the works of Jesus."[85] Following Christ's visible and glorious return, "His rule and reign will be fulfilled in the new heavens and new earth ... in which righteousness dwells and in which he will forever be worshipped".[86]

This theology identifies important non-negotiables for a church planting movement. It focuses identity and nurtures the truth. It protects against heresy and idolatry, and contains an expectation of suffering and hardship in a fallen world. It also tells God's meta-narrative: that through the whole of Scripture, God is King, reigning through his kingdom. Williams expressed it collectively, "As we confess our faith and are

---

[83] Wright, *Surprised by Hope*, 217.
[84] Jackson, *The Quest for the Radical Middle*, 399.
[85] Ibid., 400.
[86] Ibid., 400.

caught up in its story, it enlivens our worship and becomes a weapon in our warfare, to bring down Satan's kingdom, to subvert this world's systems, and proclaim that 'Jesus alone is Lord'".[87]

The Challenge of the Christian Message

How arrogant to think that just one religion is right and superior to all the others. Not only is it arrogant, it is narrow, dangerous and the cause of much world unrest. So says a commonly expressed view of religion.

Religion is believed to be one of the main barriers to peace on earth, and this elicits a number of responses. Timothy Keller identifies three of these in his book, *The Reason for God*.[88] There are calls to outlaw religion altogether, condemn religion or to insist on it being privatised. But, as Keller points out, none of these approaches works. Attempts to outlaw religion tend to make it stronger and this approach has largely been discredited. Condemning religions is seen to be "narrow". "It is no more narrow to claim that one religion is right than to claim that one way to think about all religions (namely that all are equal) is right. We are all exclusive in our beliefs about religion, but in different ways."[89] To insist that religion is kept private contradicts the very essence of what it is. Religion is a set of beliefs that explain what life is all about and what is most important. It is a "world view" and therefore it is impossible for those who hold those views to put aside those convictions when coming

---

[87] Williams, "Why Vineyard".
[88] Timothy Keller, *The Reason for God: Belief in an Age of Scepticism*, (London: Hodder & Stoughton, 2008), 5f.
[89] Ibid., 13.

God's Mission in His World

into the public square.

In our world the Christian message can sound like an arrogant imposition. However, this issue is of critical importance for missiology. It determines the extent of mission. If all religions lead to God, then presumably we divvy up the world between the religions and encourage one another to enjoy our own faiths. Christians themselves can be less than clear on this subject. What is the relation between Christianity and other faiths?

Theological responses

The traditional classification of pluralist, exclusivist, or inclusivist is used by Newbigin. These describe the three broad positions taken on the relation of Christianity to the other religions.[90] The pluralist view is the belief that the differences between the religions are not a matter of truth and falsehood, but of different perceptions of the one truth. The strictly exclusivist position holds that all who do not accept Jesus as Lord and Saviour are eternally lost. The inclusivist position, using Karl Rahner's concept of "anonymous Christianity", acknowledges Christ as the only Saviour, but affirms that his saving works extend beyond the bounds of the visible church.[91] The idea that non-Christian religions are vehicles of salvation has become widely accepted.

Newbigin himself proposes an exclusivist position in affirming the unique truth of the revelation in Jesus Christ, but inclusivist by not denying the possibility of the salvation of the

---

[90] Lesslie Newbigin, *The Gospel in a Pluralistic Society* (London: SPCK, 1997), 171f.
[91] Karl Rahner, *Theological Investigations,* Vol. 5, quoted in Newbigin, *The Gospel in a Pluralistic Society,* 174.

Uncomfortable Growth

non-Christian. It is inclusivist in that it refuses to limit the saving grace of God to the members of the Christian church, but exclusivist by rejecting that aspect which regards the non-Christian religions as vehicles of salvation. For Newbigin, salvation is pluralistic in the sense of acknowledging the gracious work of God in the lives of all human beings, but he rejects that which denies the uniqueness and decisiveness of what God has done in Christ. As Father Raniero Cantalamessa once said, anyone who is in heaven will be there because of Jesus.

This discussion draws us back to Christology. Jesus is a historical figure, and there is nothing in other religions to correspond with his incarnation as the Son of God or his atoning death on the cross for the sins of the whole world. It is not, therefore, simply that the gospel of Jesus offers us a religious option that can outdo other religions. The difference is found in the reality that salvation is by grace, through faith in Christ alone. It is this scandal of particularity that lies at the heart of Christianity. It proclaims a distinctive Christ-centred approach.

The Bible provides the framework for this Christ-alone approach:

1. All human beings, apart from the intervention and mercy of God, are perishing;
2. Human beings cannot save themselves;
3. Jesus Christ is the only Saviour.

These three biblical truths are found throughout the Scriptures and also find expression in one of the best known biblical texts: "God so loved the world that He gave his one and only Son that whoever believes in him shall not perish but have eternal life" (John 3:16). If there is only one Saviour, there can only be one way of salvation.

Jesus himself expressed it unequivocally, "No-one comes to the Father except through me" (John 14:6). Jesus does what no-one else can do. If we dethrone him, we enthrone something or someone else. Furthermore, the Bible says that this gospel is for all and that it will reach into every place and culture; hence Jesus' command, "to go into all the world" and the apostles' diligence in obeying that directive. Paul, for example, says, "God gave me the privilege of being an apostle ... in order to lead people of all nations to believe and obey" (Romans 1:5). For Paul, the Jew, it was a defiant, almost culturally traitorous act, that he now saw and accepted God's inclusiveness in Christ as something for the whole world.

Mission and Spiritual Transformation

Mission and spiritual transformation go together. There is a necessary and even indispensible connection between the two. Leaders may fear, sometimes with good justification, that by emphasising personal transformation the church might become inward looking and lose sight of its outward mission. However from a biblical perspective our spiritual growth is to go hand in hand with our service to the world.

In Jesus' life, mission and transformation are part of a whole. In fact it is precisely as Jesus' followers involve themselves in ministry that the opportunity for more transformation takes place. In Mark 9, for example, the disciples are reaching out to a boy oppressed by an evil spirit, but find they are unable to help him. The ensuing argument with the boy's father, and probable embarrassment, led the disciples to question Jesus privately in order to learn and grow (Mark 9:14–29). They undoubtedly experienced more spiritual growth through the whole episode.

Spiritual transformation will always integrate the three fundamental realities – God, the world, and the church community (see Figure 5).

Figure 5. Mission and Transformation

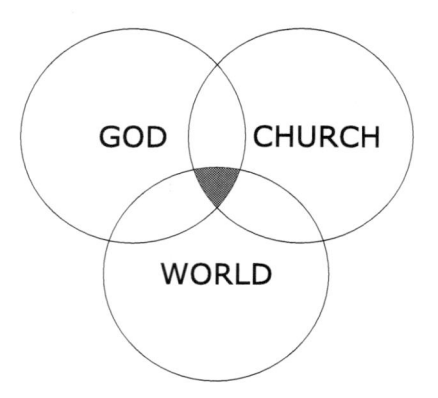

It is at the centre of the diagram (shaded area) that the conditions for both spiritual transformation and mission are found. This is where biblical discipleship happens. A relational church community becomes missionally equipped to go into the world through engagement with God and his gospel. God, by his Spirit, changes the world through us, and at the same time changes the "world" within us. The shaded area is a place of tension for us, but if we move outside it we find ourselves in altogether different "spiritualities" as represented in Figure 6.

God's Mission in His World

Figure 6. Other Spiritualities

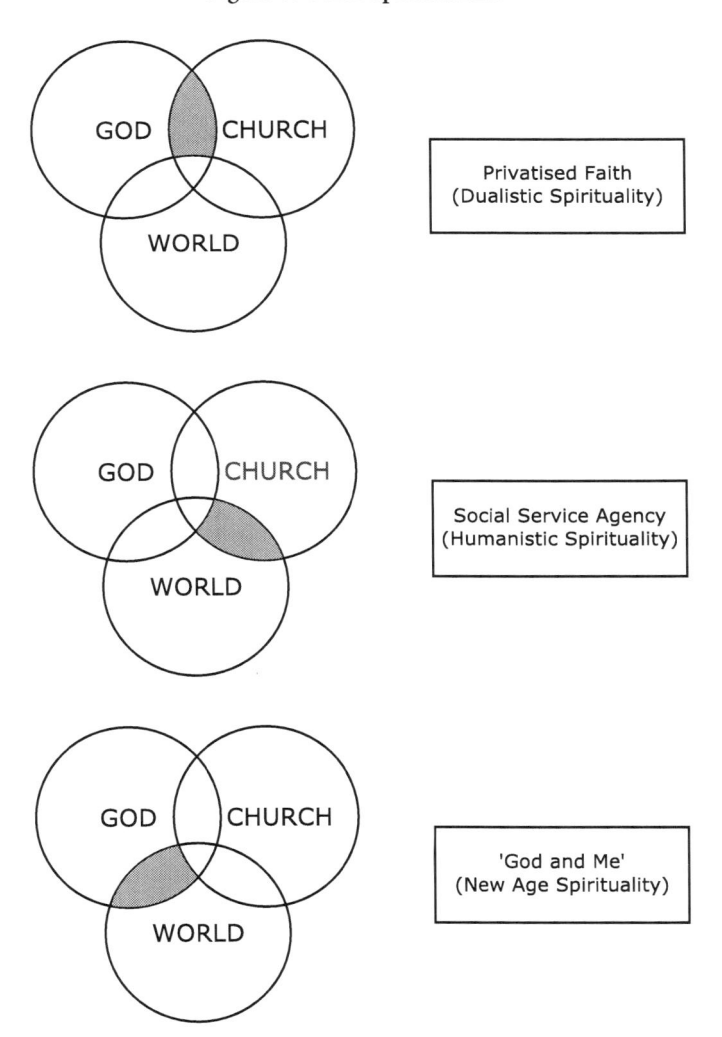

Privatised Faith
(Dualistic Spirituality)

Social Service Agency
(Humanistic Spirituality)

'God and Me'
(New Age Spirituality)

Uncomfortable Growth

A private expression of faith is, at best, practised with like-minded people in a church on Sunday. God is not understood as being active in the world through them; they keep their faith to themselves.

The church, acting as a social service agency, reaches out to the world through good causes, but is detached from God and the gospel.

"God and me" represents the many varieties of popular spirituality common today, where people interact with "god" in their own way, but bypass the gospel and church.

These "spiritualities" remind us how easily we can drift from what Christ commissioned. The church must not allow itself to become what the world says it should be, nor what we ourselves think would be best. God's intention is clear – the church is his new community, with new life and new values, pointing the world to Jesus. Like yeast, the church unsettles what is around it, changing it from within. We are always gathering, in order to scatter back into the world. As John Calvin said, it is the first duty of the Christian to make the invisible kingdom visible.

The Bible knows only of mission, which is God's from start to finish – it's a mission spanning creation and redemption. Biblical theology and doctrine always bring us back to God's saving mission through his Son, the Lord Jesus Christ. He alone is Lord and King, and it is his good news that will transform the world. Amazingly, it is as followers of Jesus participate in God's mission that they experience God at work, changing them (personal transformation) while at the same time changing the world around them (mission).

CHAPTER SIX

God's Activity through His Church

The Significance of the Church

I have suggested that the church (ecclesiology) should be a fluid doctrine, meaning that its shape and form will be determined by Jesus (Christology) and his mission (missiology). In saying this I do not wish to communicate a low or meager view of the church. To the contrary, I want to acknowledge, with a certain degree of amazement, that God has chosen the church community to be his instrument.

In Matthew 16, Jesus makes it clear that the church is an expression of divine power on earth, the primary place where the kingdom of heaven impacts the kingdom of this world. It will be able to overcome evil: "The gates of Hades will not overcome it" (v.18). Indeed, the church would so incarnate God's good news message that Jesus went on to say to Peter, "I will give you the keys of the kingdom" (v.19) to unlock God's grace to a desperately needy world. This is Jesus' view of the significance and influence of the church, the community that he promised to build (v.18).

What led to this remarkable affirmation of the church? It was Peter's profession that Jesus was "the Christ, the Son of the Living God" (v.16). Jesus makes it very clear that this was not a human discovery by Peter, but a gift of revealed grace from God, "this was not revealed to you by man, but by my Father in heaven" (v.17). It is sometimes taught that Jesus assigned Peter as the "rock" on which he would build his church. However, six verses later, when Peter denied that Jesus must suffer and die, Jesus called Peter "Satan!" (v.23). So, Peter was the "rock" when he affirmed the gospel (that Jesus was the Son of God), but he became "Satan" when he denied the gospel (that Jesus must suffer and die). It seems that the "rock" on which the church will be built was not Peter himself, but the affirmation of Jesus as God's good news. As the church proclaims and lives this good news, the transforming power of God's kingdom is known to the world.

The church: A visible body

John Stott in his book, *The Living Church,* refers to Christianity without the church as a "grotesque abnormality". The core of biblical history is the story of the calling of a visible community to be God's own people. We see this in the Old Testament with the calling of Israel, and expanded in the New Testament into all nations, gathered by Jesus into the body of Christ. Jesus didn't leave behind a book, creed, or rule of life but a band of disciples. Ephesians tells us that this redeemed community is central both to the gospel and to history, "His intent was that now, through the church, the manifold wisdom of God should be made known to the rulers and authorities in the heavenly realms" (Ephesians 3:10). At Pentecost, Peter summoned the crowd to not only repent and believe, but also be baptized and be "added" to the new community of the Spirit (Acts 2:40–47). A transfer from one community to another was clearly envisaged from the beginning.

The New Testament writers used the interesting word *ekklesia* for the church. There were a considerable number of words available in the contemporary vocabulary of that Hellenistic world to describe religious groups of people. But in the first five centuries of the Christian church we never find those other words used. They chose *ekklesia*, the secular word for the assembly of all the citizens, to describe the visible gathering of God's people. Paul always uses this word as the assembly of *God*. It is God's church. It derives its character not from its membership but from its *head*; not from those who join it but from *him* who calls it into being.

The Essential Task of the Church

Some see the church in purely functional terms. However, the church cannot fulfil the purpose entrusted to it if that is the extent of its vision. It is a "sign, instrument and foretaste" of God's reign in the place where it is called to serve, as helpfully described by Lesslie Newbigin.[92]

First, the church is to be a "foretaste" of the kingdom. Therefore it will be different from the world. If it isn't, something is wrong. It should be apparent in the church that a person has stepped from one jurisdiction into another. In so far as the church is a foretaste, it is also to be an "instrument" of the kingdom. Jesus' message was that the kingdom of God is at

---

[92] Lesslie Newbigin, *Missionary Theologian: A Reader*, compiled by Paul Weston (London: SPCK, 2006), 38.

hand. When people are impacted by the words and deeds of Jesus through his church, then the reign of God is upon them. The church is also a "sign" of the kingdom because it points to something that is not yet visible. Some aspects of the kingdom are still over the horizon. We point to a reality beyond what we can see.

When we understand the church as foretaste, instrument and sign, we more deeply realise that the gathered and going people of God play a part in making the gospel comprehensible. The church community, through its life and activity, reveals to the world God's good news.

Called to mission

Many believe that mission is the primary calling of the church. This is simplistic as mission undertaken in isolation from worship will be devoid of God-centred adoration and power, and will inevitably degenerate into human-centred activity. Jesus links the two: to "love the Lord your God with all your heart and with all your soul and with all your strength and with all your mind," and to "love your neighbour as yourself" (Luke 10:27). Worship and mission go together. The church is called to worship a missionary God. The ultimate goal of God's mission is that, "every tongue confess that Jesus Christ is Lord, to the glory of God the Father" (Philippians 2:11). This is Paul's glorious doxology of mission.

As local congregations reach out in mission to the world they will become what they already are, God's missionary people. This is Charles Van Engen's thesis, in his book, *God's Missionary People*. New church vitality and life only comes, he writes, "as they understand the missiological purposes for which they alone exist, the unique culture, people, and needs of their context, and the missionary action through which they alone will discover their own nature as God's people in God's world."[93]

Some, however, believe the church is so flawed that it is a hindrance to mission, and feel that they need to apologise for, and distance themselves from, the church. It is claimed that people "like Jesus" but not the church. There can be no denying that, at times, those within churches have seriously hurt and disappointed others. The church's reflection of Jesus and his kingdom grace is a long way from the mark. But, God chooses to use flawed people, which is another way of saying that he uses people. Unflawed people don't exist.

God's design for the church is underlined by Stott, observing from the book of Acts that "The Lord didn't add people to the church without saving them, and he didn't save them without adding them to the church". When people lose sight of the depth and sharpness of Jesus and his gospel they seem to become increasingly disillusioned with the church. "And once they leave the church they've left the only institution whose mission aims for eternity, and whose gospel is truly good news."[94] God's revelation of Jesus determines the church's mission. Jesus made his mission the model for ours, saying, "As the Father has sent me, I am sending you" (John 20:21). We love. We go. We serve. We follow in Jesus' footsteps.

---

[93] Charles Van Engen, *God's Missionary People: Rethinking the Purpose of the Local Church* (Grand Rapids, MI: Baker Books, 1991), 20.
[94] Kevin de Young and Ted Kluck, *Why We Love the Church: In Praise of Institutions and Organized Religion* (Chicago, IL: Moody Publishers, 2009), 51.

Diversity and Unity in the Church

There is no greater supporter of cultural and ethnic diversity than God himself. The Bible tells us that God *planned* cultural diversity. Revelation's glimpse into heaven should remind us of that fact. There we have the picture, not of one or two nations, or even many nations, but a vast multitude from every nation, tribe, people and language gathered around the throne (Revelation 7:9). Seemingly, our cultural diversity is celebrated in heaven. Christ *redeemed* our intended oneness with all its glorious diversity.

In Galatians, Paul explains how the three historic divisions of humanity: race, class and gender are removed, so that we all become one in Christ Jesus (Galatians 3:28). The Holy Spirit *enables* unity in diversity. "By making every effort to keep the unity of the Spirit through the bond of peace", unity and diversity can be lived out in the church (Ephesians 4:2–6). As Erwin McManus, lead pastor of Mosaic Church in California, writes, "Every step the church of Jesus Christ takes to bring people of different cultures and colours together, no matter how incremental or insignificant it seems, will be like a light in the midst of darkness".[95]

Ethnic diversity

George Yancey, in his book, *One Body, One Spirit*, presents a compelling case for encouraging ethnically diverse churches.[96] Drawing extensively on the first ever US National Study of Multi-Racial Congregations, he uncovers seven factors com-

---

[95] McManus, *An Unstoppable Force*, 54.
[96] George Yancey, *One Body, One Spirit: Principles Of Successful Multiracial Churches* (Downers Grove, IL: InterVarsity Press, 2003).

mon to these churches. These factors are not altogether surprising, and include such things as culturally diverse leadership, being intentional about welcoming and reaching different people groups, and establishing church plants in mixed rather than mono-cultural communities.

Some have argued that multi-ethnic churches are not worth the effort to create and sustain. Two major arguments have been used to support this position: a church growth argument, and an argument related to cultural pluralism. The church growth perspective emphasises the creation of churches where potential members will be comfortable. One of the ways of developing this, it is argued, is to target a mono-culture which shares as many similarities as possible. Leaving aside the questions this raises for an authentic gospel ministry, a church of culturally similar people can be no guarantee of harmonious comfort!

Mono-cultural churches can be helpful in ministering to first generation immigrants where language and culture are alien. However, in our world with its increasing diversity, mixed churches would seem better suited to reach these communities. Evidence supports this, with multi-ethnic churches in the US more likely to have grown over the past year than mono-cultural churches.[97] This is not to say that all churches *must* be ethnically mixed. This will largely depend upon the location and social context of the church's ministry.

The argument from cultural pluralism seeks to lift up, and safeguard, the distinctiveness of different cultures. But, we must remember, all cultures have their weaknesses as well as strengths, and all need to be transformed by the gospel. The church's mission is not to safeguard cultural purity, but to become God's new people who love and serve the world.

---

[97] Ibid., 35. Drawing on research from the Lilly study.

Church Planting as a Missional Vehicle

Biblical support

The relevance of church planting lies in its very specific missional dynamic. As a consequence it has application for every church even if "church planting" is not on the church's agenda. Church planting is a particular activity of God through his church and has important dynamics at work, to be embraced by all missionally concerned churches.

There are many reasons for planting new churches in the UK today. Most church planters wish to base their strategies on biblical foundations. Murray argues that church planting would be a valuable contemporary expression of mission even if it had no biblical precedent. He contends that, "Many other aspects of evangelism and church life flourish without explicit biblical endorsement."[98] He cites examples such as the Alpha Course and evangelistic guest services. His point is to distinguish between two different uses of the New Testament in relation to church planting. For those who have already established church planting practices, they may be in danger of using the Bible simply as a justification for what they have already done. Others are interested in finding guidelines for church planting and will undoubtedly draw inspiration, perspective, and resource for their thinking from the Bible.

The New Testament details the mission of the earliest churches in a world that had no churches. Throughout history, pioneer evangelism into virgin territory around the world has involved the planting of new churches. Our context is different, as churches have existed in Britain for many centuries. How-

---

[98]George Yancey, *One Body, One Spirit: Principles Of Successful Multiracial Churches* (Downers Grove, IL: InterVarsity Press, 2003), p.62.

ever, with 90% of the population having little or no meaningful connection with the church, planting new churches, as well as renewing existing ones, has to be a priority.

Church planting and the book of Acts

The book of Acts contains a wealth of material giving perspective to contemporary church planting. This is not to say that Acts is simply a church planting manual, as this would fail to recognise the author's purpose, or do justice to the breadth of his interests. Nevertheless, it is an extraordinary account of explosive church planting, and there are considerable lessons to be learnt.

Acts covers a period of about thirty years, from Jesus' ascension to Paul's imprisonment in Rome. Just three short decades, half a life-time, and the good news had travelled and been planted all the way from Jewish Jerusalem to gentile Rome. Luke records this movement and growth in six geographical expansions, each section concluding with a similar summary verse underlining the increase and growth, "So the word of God spread. The number of disciples in Jerusalem increased rapidly, and a large number of priests became obedient to the faith" (Acts 6:7 cf. 9:31, 12:24, 16:5, 19:20, 28:31).

Luke's point and central message is clear: this gospel, empowered by the Holy Spirit, is unstoppable! At the same time, we are told, there were huge challenges and sacrifices in this church planting mission. It is often assumed, for example, that the twelve apostles were the pioneers, constantly pushing forward in evangelising the world.[99] However, in the first half

---

[99]Martin Garner, *A Call for Apostles Today,* Grove Evangelism Series, Ev 77 (Cambridge: Grove Books, 2007), draws the distinction between Luke's use of apostles as restricted to the twelve, and Paul's

Uncomfortable Growth

of Acts it was others, such as Stephen and Philip who, whilst commissioned to wait on tables, were highly involved in evangelising (Acts 6:8–7:60, 8:4–40). Persecution then released many unknown disciples from Jerusalem and the expansion began in earnest (Acts 8:1–3). In the second half of Acts, Luke concentrates on Paul's expansive mission and his anchoring of the faith in every place through the churches he planted.

Some church planting lessons and realities are worthy of note.

1. A "beachhead" was established through the development of the church in Jerusalem. Establishing that first presence, together with the necessary foundations, took time (Acts 1–7).
2. Gospel mission was a deep conviction from the very beginning. Jesus' command was ringing in their ears and now in their hearts (Acts 1:8). Planting church communities was, for them, the only way of making disciples.
3. Receiving the gift of the Spirit was understood to enable everyone to be witnesses ("all people", Acts 2:17). The empowering and mobilisation of all followers was crucial in planting churches.
4. Different churches apparently had different callings. Three "base" churches seem to have emerged in key strategic cities – Jerusalem, Antioch and Ephesus. These churches seem to have provided particular training and resources for the church planting mission (e.g. Acts 13:1–3).
5. There was an insistence on the cross-cultural dimension of the church's mission. This was to go "to the ends of

---

use of the term in which it is never in reference to the twelve.

the earth" (Acts 1:8), and would include people from all nations. These early followers of Jesus faced the challenge of differentiating between those aspects of the good news which were biblically essential, and those which were sociologically negotiable (Acts 15).

Church planting and the epistles

Newly planted churches need teaching and encouragement. Many of the New Testament letters are sent from leaders to the young church plants. 1 and 2 Timothy and Titus are examples of such letters from Paul to team members in Ephesus and Crete respectively. They contain spiritual and practical guidance that every contemporary church planter and leader would want to know. These include the recognition and appointment of local leaders, the foundations that need to be laid in the churches, the development of appropriate worship, teaching and pastoral care. Even Paul's great letter to the Romans is not just to be seen as a theological treatise, but also as a deeply practical teaching for establishing healthy churches.

As already noted, cross-cultural issues were high on the agenda of the New Testament planting mission. In particular, did Gentile believers have to (effectively) become Jews with respect to customs and observances? Many of these things, such as commitment to the Sabbath, distinguished them from the pagan world. But were these necessary for salvation? Up until this mission expansion, these questions had never arisen. The letters to the Romans and Galatians expounded theologically the conclusion reached by the Council of Jerusalem that, "we should not make it difficult for the gentiles who are turning to God" (Acts 15:19). In Galatians, chapter 3, Paul showed how even Abraham was saved by faith, rather than through observance, "He believed God and it was credited to him as righteousness" (v.6). God had "announced the gospel in advance" to him (v.8). Furthermore, the Law did not come until 430 years later (v.17), clearly indicating that it was not the basis for salvation. The gospel promise was already spoken to Abraham and his seed (v.16).

In addition to cross-cultural issues, the New Testament letters provide in-depth teaching on many subjects including lifestyle issues, tending and mending relationships, persevering through hardship and understanding what is yet to come.

Church planting and the gospels

The gospels provide a primary source of inspiration for church planters and leaders. Ultimately, it is Jesus himself who teaches us about these things. The gospels can be read as mission documents, articulating the life and ministry of Jesus. His teaching is about wealth, violence, and power; the building of relationships that are open, honest and faithful to the highest standards, whilst being realistic about failure; a community that balances individual responsibility and the call to be together; and a leadership which is entirely different from the world. If there has been a tendency towards studying the epistles at the expense of the gospels, it has been to the church's detriment. There should be no polarisation between gospels and epistles. They are complementary, but differ in form and content. Both the New Testament letters and the gospels were intended to help various early church communities to develop as followers of Jesus.

Jesus demonstrates, with his own followers, how to make disciples. It is all there, and he is the Master of it. Disciple-making lies at the heart of church planting, and church life generally, so we must return to Jesus and learn afresh with new eyes. The gospel accounts of Jesus sending out the twelve (Matthew 10) and then the seventy-two (Luke 10) are packed with adaptable lessons for church planters.

Church planting in the UK

Two particular contributions of church planting as a vehicle for mission are significant for the UK context. In the first place, church planting is congruent with the New Testament church in recognising that new believers must be incorporated into church communities. As such, church planting and the missional dynamics of planting should always be a strategic option for making disciples and experimenting with new approaches.

The New Testament recognises ministry to people groups as well as to individuals. Jesus related to tax collectors, prostitutes, the poor, the pharisees and children. In the book of Acts, the advance of the gospel is measured not only geographically, but also in terms of new groups of people (e.g. priests Acts 6:7; God-fearers Acts 10:2; Greeks Acts 11:20, 17:12; and gentiles Acts 13:46).

Secondly, church planting understanding holds that churches are, by nature and definition, reproductive. The planting imagery resonates with this possibility of multiplication. Church growth is often likened to the growth of a living organism. Living things look for ways to reproduce themselves, and are not simply concerned with their own growth. The ability of churches to reproduce fresh expressions of kingdom life lies at the heart of church planting.

The planting of new churches comes out of deeply held convictions about the significance of the church to the purposes of God in the world. It has the privilege of seeking to shape the church for today. Murray writes, "At its best, church planting has the capacity to both recall the church to its primary task of mission and to remind mission strategists of the significant role of the church."[100]

To Sum Up

We can be in no doubt that God is fully aware of the shortcomings and sin of his people, the church. Yet despite this, he has chosen it as his instrument; an instrument to demonstrate, albeit imperfectly, a community which is rich in diversity, unity and love. A church that goes into the world to serve, pointing to Jesus and not itself. The planting of a wide variety of churches must be part and parcel of God's activity through his people.

The New Testament transforms a massive missionary idea into energetic missionary praxis. Jesus launched a movement that aimed at the ingathering of the nations. So, as we move to Part Three, we consider the fundamental Christian practices of making disciples, developing leaders and planting churches.

Discussion Questions on Theology

1. What provides the basis of how you and your church do life and ministry? Is it church programmes? Is it your mission? Or is it based on Jesus himself? Review Figure 4. How in practice do you ensure you start in the right place with the right questions? For study: Matthew 5:28–34.
2. It has been said that nothing is more apparent today than our inability to live as we know we should. The ingredi-

---

[100]Murray, *Church Planting*, 60.

ents of Christian transformation (the gospel, the Spirit and spiritual disciplines) are presented on p.68–78. How are you and your church applying each of these "ingredients"? For study: Romans 1:1–17. What is the gospel? (v.1–4) What do we do with the gospel? (v.5–15) What does the gospel achieve? (v.16,17)

3. Figure 5 suggests that Christian mission will always find itself where God, church and world overlap. By contrast, Figure 6 indicates how easily we can end up in some other place. What can be done to more firmly place yourself and your church in the centre of God's activity?

Recommended Books on Theology

1. Lesslie Newbigin, *Missionary Theologian: A Reader*, compiled by Paul Weston (London: SPCK, 2006). A comprehensive compilation of Newbigin's theological and missiological themes drawn from his many books and articles.

2. Tom Wright, *How God Became King: Getting to the Heart of the Gospels* (London: SPCK, 2012). A book focussing on the gospels, kingdom and cross.

3. Christopher J.H. Wright, *The Mission of God: Unlocking the Bible's Grand Narrative* (Nottingham, UK: Inter-Varsity Press, 2006). An exceptional biblical presentation of the God of mission, the people of mission and the arena of mission.

PART THREE

PRACTICE

CHAPTER 7

Jesus Made Disciples

An Inspiring Example: Dietrich Bonhoeffer

Above the great west door of Westminster Abbey are ten statues of martyrs of the church. Not historically distant figures from the early centuries, but martyrs of the twentieth century. One of those honoured is Dietrich Bonhoeffer, the German theologian, writer and pastor. I well remember being moved when I first saw this statue, as I had come to admire Bonhoeffer as one of the most significant lives of the twentieth century.

He had a very privileged upbringing, was well travelled and very well educated. He was, at twenty-one, a doctoral graduate, and at twenty-three, the youngest person ever appointed to a lectureship in Systematic Theology at the University of Berlin, in 1929. His contemporaries saw his career as glittering. He was insightful and didn't pull his punches! On his first visit to America he wrote of the church: "In New York they preach about virtually everything; only one thing is not addressed, or is addressed so rarely that I have as yet been unable to hear it, namely, the gospel of Jesus Christ, the cross, sin and forgiveness, death and life." His assessment of seminary life, on the same visit, was no more complimentary: "There is no theology here ... the students – on the average 25 to 30 years old – are completely clueless with respect to what dogmatics is really about. They are unfamiliar with even the most basic questions."[101]

He was a man of faith. He was a man of reason. But above all he was a man of action, who wrote prophetically in 1937, two years before the outbreak of World War Two, that "When Christ calls a man, he bids him come and die." For Bonhoeffer, following Christ, whatever the personal cost, meant resisting and speaking out against the Nazi State and its awful evilness. Just three weeks before the end of the war, Bonhoeffer was hanged by the SS at Flossenburg Camp because of his complicity in the plot to assassinate Adolf Hitler. His perspective on death as a Christian was robust. In a sermon he preached, while a pastor in London (1933), he said: "No-one has yet believed in God and the kingdom of God, no-one has yet heard about the realm of the resurrected, and not been homesick from that hour, waiting and looking forward joyfully to being released from bodily existence." He went on, "Death is grace, the greatest gift of grace that God gives to people who believe in Him."[102]

Bonhoeffer's was a muscular Christianity. He understood the cost of discipleship and lived it. Though a theologian, he was a passionate discipler. His "under the radar" seminary in Germany for training young men, had a great emphasis on spiritual disciplines, prayer, use of the Bible and learning to

---

[101] Quoted in Eric Metaxas, *Bonhoeffer, Pastor, Martyr, Prophet, Spy* (Nashville, TN: Thomas Nelson, 2010), 99–101.
[102] Ibid., 531.

live together. In many ways his training appeared as an "old" discipleship for a new world. His life, legacy and example have much to say to Western Christianity's current circumstances.

Discipleship: Its Nature and Challenge

Discipleship is not easy. This is true of both *being* a disciple and *making* disciples. G.K. Chesterton put it like this: "Christianity has not so much been tried and found wanting, as it has been found difficult and left untried."[103] It involves the call to live in a diametrically different way to the world around us. The culture's counterfeit values are everywhere: the worship of celebrity, affluence, popularity and success. However, we need look no further than our own hearts. When we do we see the "mixture" and evidence of the yet-to-be converted areas in our own lives. Discipleship is uncomfortable growth. This reality about the experience of discipleship needs to be kept in mind as we think about this primary task of making disciples.

Defining discipleship

Let's be clear about what we are aiming for. Jesus' words recorded at the end of Matthew's Gospel, and echoed in each of the other three gospels (Mark 16:15–18, Luke 24:46–49, John 20:21–22) are rightly recognised as the church's mission for all time: "Therefore go and make disciples of all nations, baptising them in the name of the Father and of the Son and of the Holy Spirit, and teaching them to obey everything I have commanded you. And surely I am with you always, to the very end of the age" (Matthew 28:19–20). Brilliant in its simplicity, but strangely ignored by much of the church, this commission-

---

[103]Quoted in Willard, *The Spirit of the Disciplines*, 1.

ing of the first disciples was passing on to them and all followers down through history the unique ministry that Jesus had made possible.

Jesus never failed to lose sight of his prime directive: to seek and to save those who are lost (Luke 19:10). This being the case, it is not surprising to find the noun "disciple" appearing no less that 264 times in the gospels and Acts – the essential meaning being someone who becomes a life-long learner and apprentice of Jesus. David Watson expressed it simply as someone who "has committed himself (or herself) to Christ, to walking Christ's way, to living Christ's life and to sharing Christ's love and truth with others."[104]

What, however, may be surprising is how unclear about this mandate the church can be, focusing instead on a plethora of other activities and concerns. As someone once commented, when an organisation no longer knows what it is meant to be doing, it tries to do everything, and that very often rather poorly.

The unhelpful separation of evangelism and discipleship

"The greatest thing we can do for anyone is to bring them face to face with the Christ who died for them", so writes Michael Green.[105] This is an expression of the intensely personal nature of the gospel that we find in Scripture.

Perhaps the most all-embracing definition of evangelism is still that of the English Archbishop, William Temple: "To evangelise is so to present Jesus Christ in the power of the Holy

---

[104]David Watson, *Discipleship* (London: Hodder and Stoughton, 1981), 66.
[105]Michael Green, *Evangelism Through the Local Church* (London: Hodder and Stoughton, 1990), 9.

Spirit, that men shall come to put their trust in God through him, to accept him as their Saviour, and serve him as their King in the fellowship of his church." This definition makes the important point that true evangelism ushers in discipleship.

In practice, evangelism has often been disconnected from discipleship. When this happens churches experience shallowness and frustration leading to inadequate integration of people into the body for ongoing spiritual life. "The great tragedy of modern evangelism," writes Jim Wallis, "is in calling many to believe but few to obedience".[106] Jesus, in his ministry, links the two activities by talking about the "making of disciples".

The gospels give a unique glimpse of Jesus making contact with all sorts of people and bidding them to follow him on a discipleship journey. In fact it is not altogether clear at what point the twelve are converted. However, it is very clear that they became followers of Jesus and over time bore the fruit of true conversion.

Discipleship and our world

Not only has there been a separation of evangelism and discipleship, but also a focus on "making a decision" with little provision for ongoing formation. It is perhaps not surprising that the church in nations which have inherited Western approaches to Christianity is experiencing some of the same problems. Continents such as Africa and South America, which are experiencing significant evangelistic growth, also report a similar difficulty in the task of discipleship.

The church in the age of a united Christendom was able to rely on some cultural support in discipling people. Society's

---
[106] Jim Wallis, *Agenda for Biblical People* (New York: Harper Press, 1976), 23.

common life together pointed to its religious beliefs where God seemed "inevitable". The "Christianised culture" meant that instruction in the faith looked like a church membership class rather than what we would understand as discipleship training. Today our society does not point to a particular faith in God. To believe requires a conscious intentionality that Christians in the past did not know or need.

Some cultural characteristics are particularly challenging for discipleship. The huge impact of consumerism is shifting the Western world from being a culture of production to a culture of consumption. Indeed the production of goods is moving increasingly to Eastern nations such as India and China.

In this culture of consumerism, desires and wants become much more important than contributions. Increasingly, spending, eating and sensory desires are out of control. Further, the addictive nature of consumerism means that society is largely unaware of being captured by it. As one writer put it, "We (the church) have paid the culture around us the ultimate compliment: careful study and often imitation."[107] This is a far more insidious challenge to discipleship than may be at first recognized. The phenomenon of consumerism aims to manage the value and significance that people give to products and the relative status that they derive from them. Most people are profoundly susceptible to the allure of money and things. Consumerism is a far more successful promoter of unbelief than outright intellectual atheism.

One of the subtle religious appeals of consumerism is that it offers a new immediacy, a living alternative to God's reality and what is still to come. By being offered "heaven now", people give up the ultimate quest in pursuit of that which can be immedi-

---

[107] Crouch, *Culture Making*, 9.

ately consumed. As Hirsch contends, "Consumerism has all the distinguishing traits of outright paganism – we need to see it for what it really is."[108] By contrast Christian discipleship emphasises self-denial, giving rather than getting, and living in response to what God has freely given us in Christ, both now and in the future. This is a call to swim against a very strong current.

The Foundations of Discipleship

The dramatic capitulation of the German church to Hitler in the 1930s was, of course, the context for Dietrich Bonhoeffer. How could the "church of Luther", that great teacher of the gospel, have come to such a place? The answer is that the true gospel, summed up by him as "costly grace", had been lost. In *The Cost of Discipleship*, Bonhoeffer saw what he called "cheap grace" as the deadly enemy of the church. He wrote, "Cheap grace is grace without discipleship, grace without the cross, grace without Jesus Christ, living and incarnate", the justification of sin, without the justification of the sinner.[109] It is supposed that because God has paid the account in advance, everything can be had for nothing. However, real grace is costly grace, which is like the treasure hidden in the field, and for the sake of it a person will gladly go and sell all that he or she has. As Bonhoeffer explains, if we answer the call to discipleship only Jesus knows the path and the journey's end: "But we do know it will be a road of boundless mercy. Discipleship means joy."[110]

---

[108]Hirsch, *The Forgotten Ways,* 111.
[109]Dietrich Bonhoeffer, *The Cost of Discipleship* (London: SCM Press Ltd., 1959), 36.
[110]Ibid., 32.

Uncomfortable Growth

In another study of discipleship, *The Training of the Twelve*, A.B. Bruce continually grapples with the issue of how Jesus reproduced himself and multiplied his endeavours.[111] He points out that the basis of Jesus' discipleship is that followers should be with him in order to learn from him. It is the application of Jesus' practice of being with his followers that needs careful examination today. There is possibly nothing more obvious, but more neglected, than this principle.

In recent years there has been increasing interest in some older traditions of discipleship. These emphasise the importance of a personal relationship with a teacher such as a mentor or spiritual director. In his book, *The Divine Conspiracy*, Dallas Willard sets forth what he calls a "curriculum for Christlikeness".[112] It involves the correlation between three activities that are centred on the renewing of our mind through the word of God. These are: the action of the Holy Spirit; the practice of Spiritual disciplines; and the ordinary events of life, within which the first two are set. All three activities are absolutely essential and play a part in God's transformation of a person from the inside (the mind) to the outside (behaviour).

Learning from a discipler seems to fundamentally follow the way that Jesus went about things, and we are once again called back to the gospels to learn afresh from his approach. It is no coincidence that three classic books on discipleship, namely, *The Cost of Discipleship,* by Dietrich Bonhoeffer, *The Training of the Twelve,* by A.B. Bruce and *The Divine Conspiracy,* by Dallas Willard, all derive their content and inspiration from a careful

---

[111] A.B. Bruce, *The Training of the Twelve: Ageless Management Principles For Developing Competent Leadership* (Grand Rapids, MI: Kregel Publications, 1971).

[112] Willard, *The Divine Conspiracy.*

study of the gospels generally, and the Sermon on the Mount in particular.

The Discipleship Practices of Jesus

Clearly, Jesus' discipling of the twelve was unique, not only because of who Jesus was, but also because of his particular cultural setting. The task of contextualizing Jesus' methods does need doing, but requires far less adjustment than many would lead us to believe. The search for an effective discipling programme will fail unless it applies his clear biblical practices.

It is not that these practices are new or unobserved from the gospels, but rather that they are just not done. The cost in time and effort is too high. Other aspects of ministry seem more urgent. Yet in reflecting on over thirty years of ministry, I realize that these discipleship lessons learnt at the start ought to have been applied far more single-mindedly throughout my life. The secret of discipleship lies in being biblical, not only in our goals and content, but also in our methods. In order to obey Christ's command (to make disciples), we must follow His example.

The following observations from the gospels owe much to my good friend Mark Ashton, whose life as a discipler never waned.

Sharing our lives

The communication of the Christian faith involves the whole life of the communicator. It is showing in practice how the Christian life is lived. Jesus spent a great deal of time with his disciples whether it was leisure time, routine living or ministry work. When he was doing things he took his disciples with him so they could learn by watching him in action. He allowed them to see him weak and troubled (Matthew 26:36–46), forgiving (Luke 23:34), healing (Mark 8:23f.), praying (Luke 1:1), teaching (Matthew 13:36), conversing with strangers (John 4:74), and persevering with friends (Mark 10:41–42).

Jesus called his disciples to be with him (Mark 3:14) because Christian faith is to be a total way of life learnt through personal relationship and shared experiences. Jesus maximized the opportunities for life-to-life discipling. This reminds us that biblical truth is a quality of person rather than an abstract concept (John 14:6). Communication of that truth happened from one person to another, one life to another.

Extended time

Jesus' discipling of the twelve was no crash course. Interestingly, it had begun before he formally called the twelve to follow him, as they already belonged to a group associated with him (Luke 6:13). This continued in person until after the crucifixion. Because of its life-to-life quality, it relied not on a brief period of intense communication, but on an extended period of low-key communication. Learning to live the Christian life happens best this way. In sharing his life, Jesus kept nothing back. He instructed his disciples by living alongside them, to the extent that on occasions they may not even have realized that they were learning things. Jesus called his disciples individually, committed himself to them, indicating that there were no short cuts to discipling.

Focus on a few

Jesus made a clear distinction between the twelve and the wider circles of his followers (Mark 4:34). He touched the lives of a great many people. His preaching to large crowds and his winsome interaction with strangers were part and parcel of his ministry. However, he was content to make a significant impact on the lives of just a few. This must be one of the most widely ignored aspects of Jesus' ministry. Today we seem far better at conducting large visible gatherings than committing to hidden work with individuals. We forget that ten years from now there will be a relative few whom we have managed to influence and disciple deeply.

In the ministry of Jesus, and then in the Acts of the Apostles, and indeed on into the history of Christianity, we see occasions when large numbers of people wonderfully responded to the Christian message. It is at this point that the integration between evangelism and discipling must be made secure. The ongoing discipling really begins following that response to the gospel message. This is where we see Jesus giving himself to individuals. We know that both Jesus and Paul experienced the discouragement of followers turning aside and ceasing to follow (John 6:66, 2 Timothy 1:15). There are seasons of response, and also reversals. But nevertheless, over the centuries, the community of believers has grown from generation to generation. This reminds us that it is supremely God's work, but he has given us a clear pattern to follow in his Son.

The discipling pattern

Jesus provides a pattern for discipling rather than a strategy or programme. It has been helpfully described in four stages:

1. I tell: you listen,
2. I do: you watch,
3. You do: I watch,
4. You do and report back to me.

This way of learning is set in the context of a growing relationship.

It begins with telling. I tell, you listen. We start with a message in words, using Jesus' message – his words found in the gospels (Mark 1:14–15). We can, therefore, do no better than to read the Bible one-on-one with another person. This is but the start.

We may have told them about the Christian life, but they also need to see it lived. The discipler is primarily a model. I do, you watch. It involves, as it did for Jesus, modelling the life of the kingdom: how we trust; how we share kindness; how we explain and share our faith; and all the works of the kingdom. These things will only be learnt as people see them happening, as well as being told about them.

It is actually stage 3 of the four stages that is the least evident in the gospel record of Jesus' practice, but stage 4 is quite clear (Luke 9:10). These two stages imply interaction. Good discipling will always elicit enquiry. Being involved in experiences that provoke questions is foundational to discipling. The most gifted and effective disciplers I have known in my life were people who had the gift of asking good questions that caused me to think and discover new things. Integral to Jesus' pattern of discipling was the conviction that every follower was to be an ambassador of Jesus and his kingdom. The whole church is called to be ministers. One of the greatest tragedies has been to allow ministry (evangelism, teaching, pastoring, prophecy ...) to become an activity for a few.

Friends and peers

Discipleship involves change. The transformation of individuals into the image of Jesus is a path altogether different from that of the world. The experience of growing in values that are different from the culture around us, requires contemporaries and friends who, together, are on the same challenging journey. Without the support of peers and friends, who provide a new environment in which change becomes possible, it is hard, if not impossible, for a disciple to make progress.

The point of community is that we are not being asked to change alone; we can change together with others. Spiritual growth for the twelve happened in a group, not in isolation. In my own experience, the times of greatest discipleship growth were in a church youth ministry and later, in a church of young adults, both of which provided powerful Christian peer group experience clearly focused on the mission of Jesus.

While God deals with each of us as individuals, he calls us to a communal life as Christians, dependent on one another from beginning to end. Leaders can shy away from group or community discipling for fear that the group may become inward looking and lack interest in outreach. Certainly, groups need focus and teaching but I doubt if it is possible for any Christian group to be *too* committed to one another. Where a group of Christians really commit themselves to one another in love, they will start to care for one another in liberating ways. It is this kind of group that is able to reach out and welcome the outsider because it is secure in its internal relationships.

Participation and maturity

In what activities did Jesus involve his disciples? Might it be that churches try to involve people in the wrong aspects of ministry? All too often those responding to Christ are seen as ready additions to the church work force, rather than those needing equipping so that they can share their faith. Involving people in practical service does play a part in discipling. It is not wrong for them to participate in organizational aspects of church, but it is wrong for them to get the impression that this is the sum total of Christian ministry. Discipling is about equipping people for their places of work, and amongst their friends and family, to point to and express God's kingdom in word and deed.

At the same time the call to maturity is clear throughout the Bible. It is a call to completeness that only God can bring (James 1:4). This maturity involves a growth in thinking, faith and behaviour (1 Corinthians 3:1,2, 14:20; 2 Timothy 2:22). The skill lies in applying these truths practically and simply to everyday life. There will be failings and we are not to shield one another from the consequences of our mistakes, but discipleship will know what it is to walk alongside another, helping to bear the burdens, empathizing with the pain, and encouraging the learning and transformation that God is working.

It is the creative application of these practices into our own church settings that will bear discipleship fruit. Ultimately, it is God alone who knows the "fruit that will last" (John 15:16). We can do no better than to follow the example of his Son. Making disciples is what Jesus told us to do. He is the Master, so let's more fully take hold of his methods of making disciples, as well as obeying his words and his deeds.

CHAPTER 8

Building a Disciple-Making Church

Tim Chester and Steve Timmis, in their book, *Total Church,* argue that gospel and community are the two key principles that shape the way that church should be done: fidelity to the core content of the gospel, and fidelity to the primary context of a believing community. At the risk of overgeneralizing, some churches place a proper and strong emphasis on the gospel; meanwhile others emphasize the importance of community.

Each group suspects the other is weak where they are strong. The first group worry that the others are soft on truth and too influenced by post-modernism. The second group accuses the first of being too regimented for real community to develop. Chester and Timmis contend that the first will do "truth" even better by embracing the concept of community, and the second group will enrich their community by thoroughly engaging with the gospel.

The local church is to function like a breathing body. The people gather for worship, teaching and equipping (breathing in), in order to then scatter into the world as representatives of

Uncomfortable Growth

Jesus (breathing out). Gathering in order to scatter is to be the disciple-making heartbeat of every church. Both the *content* for disciple-making, and the *community* through which it happens, are the subject of this chapter.

The Content of Disciple-Making

As churches develop and grow they become more complex. However, on the basis that simplicity is one step beyond complexity, and that Jesus was the master of simplicity, we will look at his primary activities to understand the necessary content for making disciples. How can we use these activities most effectively in our own disciple-making?

Matthew's account of the calling of the first disciples (Matthew 4:18–22) is followed by a description of Jesus' three principal activities: preaching, teaching and healing. "Jesus went throughout Galilee, teaching in their synagogues, preaching the good news of the kingdom, and healing every disease and sickness among the people" (Matthew 4:23). In fact, this summary verse of what Jesus did is repeated some five chapters later (9:35), effectively creating bookends to a section of Matthew's Gospel that illustrated these three practices. These primary activities of proclamation (preaching), explanation (teaching) and demonstration (healing) are fundamental to the way that Jesus made disciples.

Sometimes proclamation or teaching came first, as in the Capernaum synagogue, and a healing followed (Luke 4:31–37). On other occasions Jesus demonstrated kingdom power and followed it with explanation, as he did after his descent from the transfiguration mount when he healed a boy and then taught (Luke 9:37–45).

Building a Disciple-Making Church

The early church faithfully reproduced these activities. We read that the apostles never stopped teaching and proclaiming the good news (Acts 5:42). But they also demonstrated that good news practically through feeding widows (Acts 6:1), and supernaturally through miraculous signs and wonders (Acts 5:12).

Jesus' three activities through the church are represented in Figure 7.

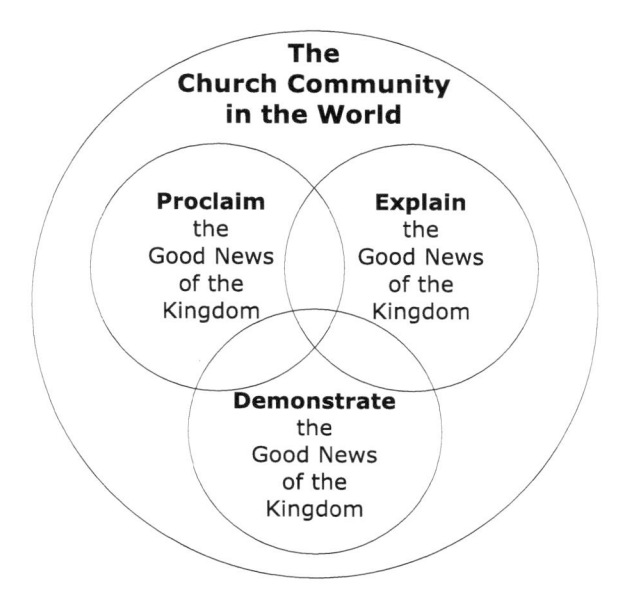

Figure 7: Disciple Making Activities

- **The Church Community in the World**
  - **Proclaim** the Good News of the Kingdom
  - **Explain** the Good News of the Kingdom
  - **Demonstrate** the Good News of the Kingdom

In the ministry of Jesus, these activities overlap in creative and God-directed ways. The outer circle of Figure 3 sets disciple-making firmly in and through the context of the church community.

Proclaiming the good news of the kingdom (preaching)

Preaching as a means of post-modern communication is often questioned. It is deemed weak and ineffective. By contrast, the New Testament underscores the word ministries of proclamation (*kerygma*) and teaching (*didache*), both of which were priorities for Jesus. The good news by its very nature demands that it is proclaimed. The word "gospel" means a news report about a life-altering event that has already happened. This news is not about what we must do, but about what has been done for us in Christ. Therefore, because the gospel is news it must be "announced"; that is what we do with news, as our news channels remind us every time we tune in.

This news is not any old news. It is news from God, not something manufactured by man (Galatians 1:1–2:5) and therefore is referred to as "the gospel of God" (Romans 1:1 c.f. Mark 1:1). Our privilege is to announce this good news regularly and faithfully, understanding that its proclamation is designed to bring people to the point of conversion. Becoming a follower of Jesus is, without doubt, a journey. But it is a journey that has crucial and definite set points. True conversion, by being born again of the Spirit (a set point), is the only way to see the kingdom of God (John 3:3–6). Proclamation of the gospel confronts people with this necessity of conversion. It is the call to go in a new direction.

The tendency to move away from proclamation surely resides in an eroded confidence in its power, and the erroneous belief that our own words and ways would be more effective. The apostle Paul would have none of it! Human wisdom will only empty the gospel of its power (1 Corinthians 1:17), while the "message of the cross" releases revelation into those whom God is saving (1 Corinthians 1:18). It is the apparent absurdity and weakness of God's message, centred in a crucified man, that ensures there can be no human boasting (1 Corinthians 1:29) and underlines that salvation is God's doing alone. It is grace from beginning to end.

Three different groups of people seem to have been attracted to Jesus: the *crowds*, the *curious* and the *committed*. The crowds contained all kinds of people, including sceptics and those who were hostile to his message. The curious wanted to know more and pressed in with further enquiry, such as Nicodemus. The committed were those who, over time, heard, believed and received Jesus and his kingdom message. Strikingly, Jesus welcomes all three categories and does not appear to have turned any away. He recognized that people were at different stages, and had absolute confidence that his gospel message had the power to draw people, in the Father's timing.

This approach of Jesus provides a model, albeit challenging, for the sort of environments we must create in our church communities. I do not want to suggest that we limit the places where proclamation takes place, because multiple settings all provide opportunities. Rather, I want to point out that within our churches regular proclamation requires discipline and courage.

Worship, as well as preaching, needs to be thought about through a missional lens. Tim Keller writes helpfully on both of these in his book, *Center Church*.[113] Why would we want to deny unbelievers access to something that is as potentially life-changing and beneficial as an experience of true worship? In the New Testament (e.g. Acts 2, 1 Corinthians 14:22–25) non-believers are attracted and disturbed by worship. From these

---

[113] Tim Keller, *Center Church,* see particularly Chapter 23 on Missional Worship and Chapter 6 on Missional Preaching.

texts we learn that: non-believers are expected in worship; are to find worship comprehensible, maybe challenging, but not boring; and any questions and puzzlement are answered in the preaching.

Preaching should be beneficial for both Christians as well as pre-Christians. Rather than spending a great deal of time preaching against the world, or calling people to try harder, preaching will show that living the life of Jesus is based upon his grace that flows from the cross, the resurrection and Pentecost. Most of all, preaching will avoid ever talking as if non-believing people are not present. If we preach to both groups it will not be long before spiritually hungry people are present. So we always preach to a "mixed" group. When we speak to pre-Christians, the Christians learn more about how to share their faith. When we speak to Christians, the pre-Christians come to see how Christianity works.

Proclaiming Jesus' good news regularly through the church's preaching will appropriately point people to the regular courses run in the church calendar which explain Christianity (Alpha, Christianity Explored etc.). These courses will communicate who Jesus is, what he has done, and how someone can come to him and enter into his life.

Explaining the good news of the kingdom (teaching)

The interplay between Jesus' preaching and teaching is quite obvious. We see it in his interactions with the crowds, the curious and the committed. So for example in Matthew 13, Jesus moved backwards and forwards between telling parables to the crowds (vv.1–3) and explaining them to his disciples in more detail (v.10f.). Later in the chapter we see the same pattern, "Then he left the crowd and went into a house. His disciples

Building a Disciple-Making Church

came to him and said, 'Explain to us the parable of the weeds in the field.' He answered ..." (Matthew 13:36). So both proclamation and explanation are essential parts in the making of disciples.

In Jesus' explanation of the Parable of the Sower he identifies why teaching is essential: "When anyone hears the message about the kingdom and does not *understand* it, the evil one comes and snatches away what was sown in his heart" (v.19). We are in a war, and there is an enemy who also battles for our lives. When the message about the kingdom is not understood the enemy takes advantage.

Jesus also makes a positive point about understanding, in speaking about the good soil: "But the one who receives the seed that fell on good soil is the man who hears the word and *understands* it. He produces a crop, yielding a hundred, sixty or thirty times what was sown" (v.23). For disciples to be made, it is not enough for them to simply hear the message, they must also come to understand it through patient explanation. As we pray and teach the Bible we know that the Spirit of God will be at work revealing truth in people's hearts. The parable tells us there will be a mixed response, for there is hard, shallow, crowded and good soil. This reality, however, does not in any way deter the sower from generously sowing seed wherever possible. He has absolute confidence that God will be at work.

What teaching content is appropriate for the making of disciples? Many church leaders (including myself) find the opening verses of Hebrews 6 salutary, "Therefore, let us leave the elementary teachings about Christ and go on to maturity" (v.1). He then proceeds to list as "elementary" teachings, which to us seem anything but elementary, such as the resurrection of the dead and eternal judgement! Nevertheless, he is insistent that followers of Jesus move on from milk to solid food, "the teaching about righteousness" (Hebrews 5:13). He is talking about increasingly living the life of Jesus, putting off the old and putting on the new. In our churches, it is worth revisiting how effectively we are teaching in our different gatherings. Teaching the Bible thoroughly Sunday by Sunday forms the backbone for the church community. Consecutive, expository teaching is the best normal diet for the whole church. Ensure that the Bible is at the heart of the gatherings that take place for children, youth, students and home groups.

A group of three people meeting together has a number of benefits for discipleship. In a busy world, they are highly flexible. People are able to arrange when and where they meet. Triplets require no expert leadership and are potentially easily reproduced. Neil Cole has written about a type of triplet, which he calls a "Life Transformation Group".[114] There is a three-fold purpose: spiritual formation, evangelistic fruitfulness and multiplication. It involves the reading of significant chunks of Scripture, accountability questions, and prayer for those the participants are seeking to reach for Jesus. The addition of a fourth person is the beginning of multiplying into two groups.

Willow Creek Community Church, with great transparency, revealed interesting findings from a survey of their own church.[115] Its leaders concluded that participation in church

---

[114]Neil Cole, *Cultivating a Life for God: Multiplying Disciples Through Life Transformation Groups* (Carol Stream, IL: Church Smart Resources, 1999).

[115]Diana Butler Bass, "Willow Creek Repents?," *God's Politics a blog by Jim Wallis and Friends,* presented by Beliefnet and Sojourners (October 2007) 1.

programmes did not inculcate Christian discipleship, and they found no observable increase in participants' love for God or their neighbour. They further concluded that Willow Creek's emphasis should be on teaching people to become "self-feeders" from God's word, and that there should be a far more thorough engagement with the spiritual disciplines.

Another way disciple-making can be strengthened is to equip and encourage, throughout the church fellowship, two Christians (often an older and a younger) to get together with an open Bible to read and apply God's word together. In these times it is natural to ask questions of the text, to get to grips with God's word and, more importantly, let it get to grips with us. These times often form a profound and life-changing relationship with another person.

A further opportunity for teaching is mid week, when, for example, a book of the Bible is taught from the front for thirty minutes before breaking into groups in order to discuss and apply the passage. Eating together prior to the teaching adds a further relational dimension, which strengthens the connectedness between people. Variations and tweaks to these ideas may well be necessary, but teaching the Bible, whether one-to-one or in groups or larger settings, is fundamental in enabling disciples to grow and feed themselves from God's word.

Demonstrating the good news of the kingdom (healing)

We now turn to Jesus' practice of healing. Healing, of course, is not the only way that the good news of the kingdom is demonstrated. The changed life of a disciple is a visible testimony to the good news. Practical acts of kindness, service to the com-

---

http://blog.beliefnet.com/godspolitics/2007/10/willow-creek-repents-by-diana.html

munity, engagement with poverty relief and action for justice, to mention but a few, are all demonstrations of the good news.

However, we cannot ignore the biblical witness to the role of healing. The gospels all record healing as a key feature of Jesus' mighty works. They do so for a very good reason. Is it not completely logical that Jesus would use healing to demonstrate the good news kingdom he was announcing? A kingdom that has an "already and not yet" dimension now and which looks forward to its completion, where disciples are assured of resurrected bodies made ready for God's new world. God is at work in healing, touching and restoring physical bodies in the present, and in doing so provides a foretaste and signpost to God's new reality, in which finally we experience a new physicality, free of pain and death.

This is the kingdom we are to deeply desire and seek; one filled with righteousness, peace and joy in the Holy Spirit (Romans 14:17) and one in which good news is preached to the poor, freedom is proclaimed to the prisoners, sight given to the blind and the oppressed are released (Luke 4:18).

In the New Testament, furthermore, there appears to be a strong connection between healing and disciple-making. The reason that this is important is because a demonstration of the good news seems to be what God so often uses, to open up the opportunity for people to hear and understand the gospel message. Early Christians shared their faith in Jesus with the confidence that God would confirm their witness "by signs, wonders and various miracles, and gifts of the Holy Spirit distributed according to his will" (Hebrews 2:4).

Church history seems to ebb and flow with times of darkness followed by spiritual renewal. A global view of Christianity over the last century reveals the re-emergence of ministry that includes a demonstration of God's power. It is an inescapable fact, from biblical study, that Jesus and the early church had a natural expectation of supernatural intervention. Jesus' message was not for the mind alone. The gospels and the book of Acts are no museum pieces. No matter how daunting healing may seem to us, it is vital that we listen and obey God's word, rather than succumb to the fear, unbelief or discouragement that may come from our own experience.

Missiologists, such as Paul G. Hiebert, challenge the Western church over its rationalism. They trace its development back to the 17th and 18th Centuries, when secularised science began explaining natural phenomena without reference to a supernatural God. The result was that our Western worldview, highly conditioned with secular humanism, was allowed to infiltrate theology and church life. It is shocking and sobering to acknowledge that the church has played a part in the secularising force in history.

The New Testament points to a relationship between the proclamation and demonstration of the good news. These two elements, time and again, go hand-in-hand in the ministry of Jesus and the early church. When Jesus sent out the twelve and then the seventy-two, the instruction was the same. For the twelve it was, "to preach the kingdom of God and heal the sick" (Luke 9:2) and for the seventy-two it was, "Heal the sick who are there and tell them that the kingdom of God is near you" (Luke 10:9). There is little doubt that people in our culture need to see that God is more powerful than the lifestyles they are serving.

How does God enable his people to connect with others and demonstrate and proclaim the good news? There are, of course, many ways. John Wimber used the language of "divine

Uncomfortable Growth

appointment", "human predicament" and "power encounter" to describe three particular connection points.

First, every follower of Jesus has what we may call "chance meetings" or unexpected openings in a conversation that seem to come out of the blue. We are not always good at seizing these opportunities, but they are "divine appointments" which God is providing. Jesus' encounter with the woman at the well, a complete stranger, is an example of such a God-arranged meeting. His spiritual insight into the woman's circumstances (a spiritual gift) and his explanation led to the woman's conversion, a mini-mission, and many coming to believe from her town (John 4:39–41).

Secondly, there is "human predicament". Nothing is simpler and more natural than offering to pray for someone who is sick or in significant need. This is what Peter does when he meets Aeneas and Tabitha in Lidda and Joppa, respectively. He compassionately prays for them, they are healed, and in both cases it caused others to believe and turn to the Lord (Acts 9:35,42). We offer to pray for those in need with the expectation that God will act, but also being content to leave the results with him.

Thirdly, a "power encounter" describes a more obvious clash of power between good and evil. Christians in non-Western parts of the world recognize this reality more readily than we do. But Satan is at work everywhere in the world, seeking to bring people into bondage and destruction. Paul's bold words to Elymas, a sorcerer in Paphos, were certainly such a power encounter. The power of God was released, the opposition was overcome, and it led to the Pro-Consul believing (Acts 13:12).

Every church will want to find ways of serving and benefiting the community. How can the good news be demonstrated in the community for its blessing? How can we become a serving people and a church that constantly turns itself outwards? As Jesus explained, in the kingdom every disciple can be great because everyone can serve (Mark 10:43); small things being done for others with great love. As Dave Workman from the Cincinnati Vineyard reminds us, Christians tend to define themselves by what they believe, but non-Christians define us by what we do. Become known in your community for being servants, rather than for what you are against. Practise radical hospitality. Over-resource outreach and evangelism in the church budget. Enable people to identify their gifting and then encourage them to use it missionally.

Natural Church Development specifies "gift-orientated ministry" as one of eight quality factors that contributes to a healthy church.[116] As people are helped to identify their gifts and skills, they can be encouraged to use those particular gifts as a bridge to mission. These are things that they can do with particular grace and in a natural way. It underlines the disciple-making contribution of all gifts. Evangelists, according to the apostle Paul, are to play a vital role in equipping all God's people for (presumably evangelistic) works of service (Ephesians 4:11–13). This growing gift awareness in God's people can be directed at encouraging everyone to play a part in demonstrating God's good news.

We move now from the content and activities of disciple-making (proclamation, explanation, demonstration) to the part that community plays in discipleship.

---

[116]Schwarz, *Natural Church Development*.

Church Community and Disciple-Making

The necessity of community

I suspect that many of us who are church leaders feel that we have been far better at acknowledging the significance of community than working it out in practice. Do we view community as a separate category from discipleship and other church priorities such as prayer and outreach? As Keller points out, community is one of the main ways we are to do outreach and discipleship.[117] The quality of our community is the real secret to fruitful ministry. He speaks about a community which goes beyond "fellowship" and which demonstrates a counter-cultural life, showing how things like money, sex and power can be used in life-giving ways. It is this sort of church community that shapes character – the people with whom we rub shoulders, converse and pray.

The busier churches become the greater is the threat to meaningful relationship. It can be seen simply as "extra" or discretionary. I heard recently the sad comment that the world does community better than the church. It is easy to generalise about shortcomings in the church. However, I think what was being referred to was the rather thin sense of relationship. In our busyness Christian community can be taken for granted.

Dietrich Bonhoeffer, in his book, *Life Together,* reminds us that living among other Christians is an immense privilege. "The physical presence of other Christians is a source of incomparable joy and strength to the believer."[118] In the final

---

[117]Keller, *Center Church*, 311.

[118]Dietrich Bonhoeffer, *Life Together: The Classic Exploration of Faith in Community* (San Francisco: Harper and Row Publishers, Inc., 1954), 19.

chapter he argues that confession provides the breakthrough in the making of community. People are destroyed by sin, but can be healed through forgiveness, acceptance and inclusion. The effect of disengagement from the community of believers is the very worst outcome for all involved. Perhaps our countless relapses into Christian feebleness are to be found in our lack of confession one to another. With this kind of confession (cf. James 5:16) strength and healing can flow into the community.

Community building is a long-term process. It is to be understood as the journeying of pilgrims seeking a better way to live and, ultimately, a better place. We don't struggle enough over what it means to be relational rather than institutional, a people rather than a place, a community rather than a meeting. Gibbs and Bolger point out, "A first century Christian would have been puzzled by the question, 'Where do you go to church?' for church was a network of people to which one belonged."[119]

Maybe it is only through the eyes of persecution that we will more fully understand biblical community. Alan Hirsch, in *The Forgotten Ways*, speaks of the need for *communitas* rather than community. By *communitas* he is referring to "the context of a shared ordeal that binds [people] together in a much deeper form of community than the one we have generally become accustomed to."[120] Drawing on anthropological studies of various rites of passage among African people groups, it is seen that individuals are driven to find each other through a common experience of ordeal. Such is the harshness of some of the initiation ceremonies that it can literally be a matter of bonding together or dying.

---

[119] Gibbs and Bolger, *Emerging Churches*, 100.
[120] Alan Hirsch, *The Forgotten Ways*, 218.

Hirsch sees this *communitas* as normative for God's people in Scripture. Examples abound: Abraham's family is called to leave and go to a place which he "knows not of"; the risk and challenge of the Exodus, where the people of Israel find themselves caught between the Red Sea and their pursuing enemy; or the flinging out of the early church into Judea and Samaria as a result of persecution. It is these instances of severe testing that provide fertile soil for disciple-making. It is precisely the experience of danger and risk that have the potential to produce a far greater degree of spiritual vigour and relational connectedness. Hirsch's point is well made. An obsession with church safety and comfort will do little for discipleship. More people than we imagine long for a mission that is challenging.

Inclusive yet distinctive

The title of Jim Petersen's book, *Church Without Walls*, expresses an important aspect of achieving an outward focussed community.[121] The church has erected barriers against the very people it is trying to reach. What unnecessary boundaries can be removed? The barriers can be cultural or religious, both of which can make connection with the world more difficult.

Social set theory identifies three ways that people gather together. First, the *bounded* or *closed* set – a social system that has clearly delineated boundaries where one either qualifies for, or is rejected from, the group. Most established institutions are predominantly bounded sets. Second, there is the *fuzzy* set, which has no real ideological centre, or boundaries for that matter. The participants are not sure what has brought them together or why they meet. Unsurprisingly, these groupings

---

[121]Jim Petersen, *Church Without Walls: Moving Beyond Traditional Boundaries* (Colorado Springs, CO: NavPress, 1992).

don't usually last very long. The third set in the theory is the *centred* set. It differs from the others in that it has a strong ideology and culture at its centre, but very few if any boundaries on its periphery. This provides a basis for community-building which can be powerfully missional.

Being loose at the edges of a centred set allows people to belong to the church community before they believe. A person is able to make a journey towards Jesus at the centre, from any distance, and from any direction. This is not to say that bounded sets are always bad and centred sets are always good. Boundaries do exist in Christianity. Salvation is a bounded set. One is either "in Christ" or not "in Christ". However, salvation is usually if not invariably a process and a journey.

Legitimate questions, though, do need to be answered about the "belong – believe – behave" continuum. Are we faithful and clear in challenging those who have joined the community to repent and believe? Is the point of decision ever reached? What happens if the pre-Christian's lifestyle adversely affects the community? A balance to these questions may be elusive but the church is to be God's new and distinctive community of people. The gospel reminds us of the ever-present tension between grace-filled truth and rule-driven practice. The *centred* set church is an attempt to be more like Jesus – inclusive yet distinctive.

Mobilising the community

Churches are to help connect Christians with the world as well as with one another. The biblical commands, to love our neighbour and live justly, and be salt and light in the world, are to motivate and guide the outward scattering of the church. Ministries of mercy, concerned with justice, relief and reform in society, as well as equipping Christians for their workplaces, are to be given resource and priority. The real challenge is not primarily about how to get people involved in the ministry of the church, but how to change things around so that the church is involved in empowering people for ministry in the world. It is thinking about how to equip and support the people of God where he has already placed them as his representatives.

By identifying a number of broad work categories within the church community – for example those involved in business, care services or education – people in similar professions can meet up to encourage one another to witness in their place of work. Prayer breakfasts, or forums for those working in the same field, can focus on equipping people. The leadership and teaching of these can be done by those who work there. Church leaders support rather than lead these gatherings, but in so doing connect with the real pressures and joys of the front line workers.

Similar to this is the concept of what has been called "communities of witness". A group of people may, for example, live together in a residential location or share a particular interest or outreach passion. Gathering together to talk and pray, they discover how they might organize themselves into a community of witness. The emphasis is on mutual support in working out the implications of mission in their particular context. These can also develop in hospitals, colleges and businesses, by identifying other Christians who work there and exploring together the opportunities for Christian ministry.

A further way of mobilizing the church might be to consider ministry in more than one location. These "mission outposts" throughout the community provide contact points for those who are unlikely to ever come to the church centre. Groups of recent immigrants, residents of a nursing home, students at college or university, or youth at a skateboard facility are all examples of possible mission outposts. These sorts of initiatives send the unmistakable message to the church – that it exists to equip people to go into the world, to value their vocation, and to be effective bearers of the good news wherever they go.

To Sum Up

"We seem to make church complex and discipleship too easy".[122] But, the aim for our churches is to be simple, accessible and equipping. We want to lower the bar of how church is done, but raise the bar of what it means to be a disciple.[123] In practice this happens through paying attention to both the content of disciple-making as well as the quality of community through which that disciple-making happens. The content of disciple-making (proclaiming, explaining and demonstrating the kingdom) is made more effective by deepening the reality of church community; and the community through which disciple-making happens is deepened the more it engages with the content of the gospel. These two things allow God to go on building a disciple-making church.

Discussion Questions on Discipleship

1. "Christianity has not so much been tried and found wanting, as it has been found difficult and left untried". How

---

[122]Hirsch, *The Forgotten Ways,* 104.

[123]For an insightful study of discipleship, see Neil Cole, *Organic Church: Growing Faith Where Life Happens* (San Francisco: Jossey-Bass, 2005).

clearly do you and your church present the call to discipleship? What inspires this kind of discipleship? For study: Luke 9:23–27.
2. The secret of disciple-making lies in being like Jesus, not only in our goals and content, but also in our methods. How can you apply more deeply the six characteristics of "method" that Jesus used? (see p.117–122)
3. For Jesus, the content of disciple-making was directed through the three activities of proclamation, explanation and demonstration, see Figure 7. List under each how you and your church are utilizing these three activities. Which of these activities that Jesus used needs to be strengthened?

Recommended Books on Discipleship

1. Tim Chester, *You Can Change* (IVP, 2008). A down-to-earth, truth-filled book on personal change.
2. Richard Rohr, *Falling Upwards: A Spirituality for the Two Halves of Life* (SPCK, 2012). Discovering transforming grace through adversity.
3. C.S. Lewis, *The Chronicles of Narnia* (London: Harper Collins, 2010). A multitude of discipleship lessons presented in the most enchanting way.

CHAPTER 9

Leadership Culture

An Inspiring Example: The Jesuits

Experience and writing from different traditions reveal insights that are hard to see in one's own tradition. Chris Lowney, in his book, *Heroic Leadership,* tells the remarkable story of the founding of the Jesuits during the Counter-Reformation.[124] Founded in 1540 by ten men, the Jesuits have had an extraordinary influence throughout the world, through the pioneering of a unique formula for moulding leaders. What particularly impresses me is the integration of love and courage, which combines and integrates relationship and task in a Christ-like way. Who, on reading the gospels, is not moved, not only by what Jesus did but also by the way he treated people? Lowney identifies four Leadership Pillars:

1. Self-awareness – the need to understand one's strengths,

---

[124] Chris Lowney, *Heroic Leadership: Best Practices from a 450-Year-Old Company that Changed the World* (Chicago: Loyola Press, 2003).

weaknesses, values and world-view;
2. Ingenuity – confidently innovating and adapting to a changing world;
3. Love – the commitment to unlock the talent, potential and dignity of others; and
4. Heroism – a willingness to question and probe one's approach, and to be energized by an appetite for risk-taking.

Leadership is understood as springing from within. It is not an act. It is life, a way of living. We never complete the task of becoming a leader. It is an ongoing process. As a consequence, all leadership begins with self-leadership and a growth in self-awareness. The story of the Jesuits, like many stories of missionary movements, makes for breath-taking reading. For Ignatius Loyola, love expressed itself in passion to see team members excel. There was a remarkable freedom from control. Their courage flowed from a godly indifference and detachment from life's idols. They testify to the fact that leadership is not the result of a dramatic defining moment, rather our defining "moment" is a pattern slowly etched through a lifetime, studded with ordinary opportunities and commitments that make a subtle difference.

Leadership in a Changing World

Developing leaders is essential for any church determined to fulfill its disciple-making mandate. But what kind of leader is required for our changing world? Might we need new priorities? Has Christian leadership got stuck in a time warp? The lyrics of the U2 song hauntingly express this perspective,

> You've got to get yourself together,
> You've got stuck in a moment and now you can't get out of it,
> Don't say that later will be better,
> Now you're stuck in a moment and you can't get out of it.[125]

One thing is clear: the future is unclear. But leadership, by its very nature, will be interested in the future. So how do we respond to the unknown? I remember learning to surf as a boy in Australia, and discovering pretty quickly that the smartest and safest thing to do was *not* to try and swim away from the waves but to head straight into them. Leadership will often feel like that.

The worst course of action to take in times of change is to bury our heads in the ground and deny that change is happening. This point is emphasised in Spencer Johnson's parable, *Who Moved My Cheese?*[126] Two pairs of mice respond differently to their environment when their cheese is moved. One pair is paralysed by the change, and they die. The other pair goes in search of a new source of cheese. The simple lesson is that change happens, and we must be bold enough to adjust and adapt.

In the middle of a swirling cauldron of change and ambiguity stands the leader. Painfully aware of personal frailty and vulnerability, he or she knows that the future demands trust.

---

[125] U2 quoted in Frost and Hirsch, *The Shaping of Things to Come*, 3. "Stuck in a Moment You Can't Get Out Of", (Jan 2001), from the album, *All That You Can't Leave Behind*, (Oct 2000).

[126] Spencer Johnson, *Who Moved My Cheese?: An Amazing Way To Deal With Change In Your Work And In Your Life* (London: Vermillion, 1999).

Uncomfortable Growth

God called Abraham to "Leave your country, your family, and your father's house, for the new land that I will show you" (Genesis 12:1). We no longer live with certainty and uninterrupted plans. Like Abraham we are called to live in a new way; not protecting what we already have, but being confident to go where God directs. Without this foundation we may well find ourselves embarrassed by *our* plans.

A Needed Change in Leadership Emphasis

Leadership is usually explored from a leader-centric perspective. After all, it is argued, leaders are the practitioners of leadership and therefore know what they are talking about. The emphasis focuses around measurable objectives, setting goals, casting vision and designing church structure.

But leadership at its most fundamental is about relationship. And like all relationships at least two parties are required – followers as well as leaders. Both play a crucial role in the relationship despite much leader-centric writing assuming that followers have little part to play. Leadership is a gift given by God, but also given by those who choose to follow. If the relational aspect of leadership is given scant attention the church community will suffer. As Viv Thomas writes in *Future Leader*, "If leaders don't lead well, then things go wrong for lots of other people. Most delight and pain in our communities and organisations can be traced back to some leader or other who shaped us directly or indirectly".[127] Recent research, cited by Walter Wright from the field of emotional intelligence, shows that the emotional-relational character of leadership is twice as

---

[127]Viv Thomas, *Future Leader* (Milton Keynes, UK: Paternoster, 1999), 1.

important as vision and strategy. This is a very striking assertion. "We influence others through vision and organisation, but the most significant influence of leadership flows through values and relationships."[128] It is, therefore, obvious that our vision and mission will be enhanced or constrained according to the health of the relational culture.

But wait a minute. Doesn't vision take precedence over relationship? From leadership tools, used to identify the relative strengths of task and relationship, the task-orientated "type A" leader is prized. Leaders do want to get things done and see things develop. The same can be true with vision and values, where vision (*what* we do) is considered the leader's *real* job, and values (*how* we do things) take a second place.

What does the Bible say? Is God more interested in us attaining our goals or in right relationships? The Bible is replete with examples of leadership, good and bad. We can, of course, learn much from books on leadership but our greatest need by far must be to hear what God has to say.

Jesus On Leadership

The single clearest teaching Jesus gave on leadership is found in Mark 10:35–45. In response to James and John's request to sit at Jesus' right and left hand in his glory, and to the indignation of the other disciples when they hear about it, Jesus calls them all together and teaches them. He said, "You know that those who are regarded as rulers of the Gentiles lord it over them, and their high officials exercise authority over them. Not so with you" (v.42–43). The twelve, and Jewish people generally, knew

---

[128]Walter C. Wright, *Relational Leadership: A Biblical Model for Influence and Service* (Downers Grove, IL, 2009), 34.

well the gentile model of authority. Ancient near-Eastern kings had long claimed to be gods and ruled tyrannically; Greek rulers had adopted the same posture through much of the Eastern Mediterranean. The Roman Emperor and his provincial rulers were viewed in much the same light.

The grace-filled church is to demonstrate an entirely different kind of leadership, one which will stretch us and involve uncomfortable growth: "Instead, whoever wants to become great among you must be your servant, and whoever wants to be first must be slave of all" (v.43–44). Jesus' words are shocking. His kingdom operates on an entirely different value system: looking out for others, serving others, becoming aware of others' needs, and lifting others up when they are weak and struggling. It seems illogical but this is how Jesus' kingdom works. It is how the power of God is released and how those we lead flourish. To underline this altogether different type of leadership Jesus, having predicted his death (v.33f), then explains his death (v.45). His death will be *exemplary*, "The Son of Man did not come to be served, but to serve" and it will also be *substitutionary*, "and to give his life as a ransom for many." So if our Lord and Master is like v.45, not coming to be served but to serve, we must certainly become like vv.43, 44, finding greatness through servanthood.

Does our church leadership look this this? Or have we done the very thing that Jesus told us not to do, to emulate the world's leadership? Influence is undoubtedly demonstrated through both these contrasting models of leadership. They both achieve "results". The world's leadership is a *structural* authority imposed from above (v.42); it achieves order and maintains control over people. The leadership of which Jesus speaks releases a *kingdom* authority expressed through the heart of a servant (v.43–44); it frees and restores relationship (v.45). It is to the cross we must go to learn about leadership, just as Jesus did with his disciples.

The leader creates the culture of the group they lead. They are the guardians of the way things are done as well as what is done. The relational culture in a church is as important as its vision. In fact it should be part of its vision. Jesus' new commandment was that we should "love one another". Ironically that is probably more challenging to do than to love our neighbour, or even our enemies. I remember Martin Peppiatt, who invited me to serve as his curate in the early 1980s, once saying words to the effect that the world is yet to see a church that fully lives the life of grace. And that comment from one of the most grace-filled people I have ever known.

Combining Values and Vision

I am arguing for a leadership that pays as much attention to the church's culture, shaped by its relational values, as is given to the mission directed by the church's vision. There will be tension; but hopefully a *healthy* tension between relationship and task, values and vision; between how we work with people and what we aim to accomplish.

Keller uses the language of success, faithfulness and fruitfulness to make a similar point.[129] The "success" lens focuses on church numbers, growing giving, and ministry expansion. The "faithfulness" criterion emphasizes the need for sound preaching, caring pastoring and godly character. But of the three, "fruitfulness" is the most biblical and helpful means of evaluating leadership. Jesus told his disciples that they were to "bear

---

[129] Keller, *Center Church,* 13–16.

Uncomfortable Growth

much fruit" (John 15:8). This includes growth in conversions, character and relationships (see Romans 1:13, Galatians 5:22). Fruitfulness combines the good we find in both success and faithfulness. Fruit speaks for itself. It is evidence of something that is healthy and wholesome.

It seems to me that we arrive at fruitfulness when leaders combine values with vision. By values, I am not referring to those non-negotiable priorities such as worship, prayer, the Bible and so on. I am talking about the way that relationships are worked out in practice, the fruit of the Spirit growing in all lives. This combining of values with vision is expressed in Figure 8.

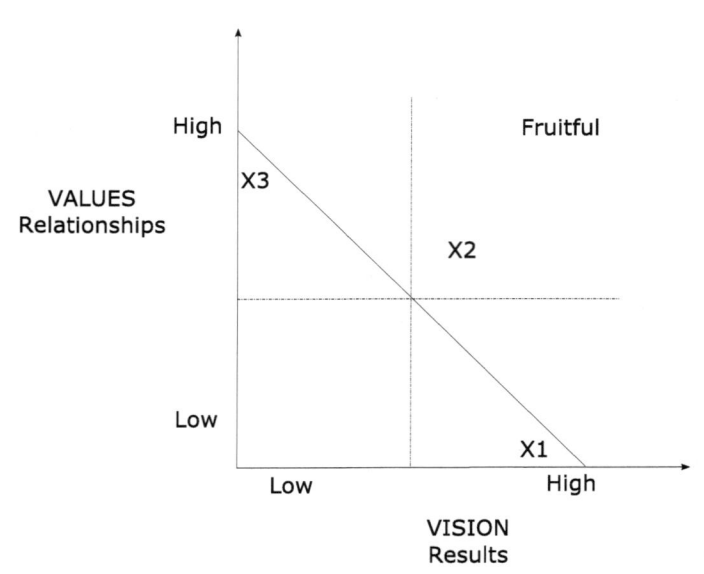

Figure 8. Values and Vision Appraisal

Leadership Culture

The top right-hand quadrant represents effective and fruitful leadership. The point represented by X1 is the leader who produces exceptional "bottom line" results but has ignored pretty much every value in getting there. As a consequence that person's leadership detracts from the overall fruitfulness of the church. Results mean little if relationships are damaged. The end does not justify the means.

Point X2 represents leaders whose results are a little less than X1 (but still exceptional), but where relational values have been highly respectful, ending up well into the fruitful quadrant.

Of course, the opposite failing is for the leader to lose connection with the vision, focusing almost exclusively on relationships (represented by point X3) resulting in a "touchy/feely" leader who is ineffectual. The point is not to excel in one at the expense of the other, but to embrace both values and vision, and thereby produce fruitfulness.

Leadership in churches is neither straightforward nor simple. Decisions taken will not always be popular. Church life requires some structural authority. Any organisation or institution requires principles and procedures. In fact people would be upset if leaders did not manage these things well. But it is our values that help us to apply the necessary structural authority in a way that does not override kingdom authority. People immediately know which authority is being exercised. The challenge is how do we honour the legitimate needs of structural leadership while creating space and priority for the grace and power of kingdom leadership?

The point of Figure 8 is that vision with insufficient attention to values can have a disproportionately negative impact. The focus shifts from "doing right things" to "doing things right". "Doing things right" will put procedures, protocol and precedents before people. This is not the way of the kingdom, and we can find ourselves being so right that we end up being wrong. This seems to be Jesus' meaning in the parable of the lost son (Luke 15:11–32). One character in the parable lives his life totally right, "by the book", but in so doing seems unable to be relationally generous like his Father. His rules (doing things right) were more important to him than restored relationships (doing right things). I very much regret the times as a leader when I have failed to make this distinction and have landed on the side of doing things right rather than right things thereby missing an opportunity to live out the Spirit of Jesus.

Daniel Goleman explains the impact of relational dynamics in his book, *The New Leaders*. His thesis is that how we handle ourselves in our relationships matters more than our I.Q. and technical skills.[130] This is what he calls "emotional intelligence" and it is at the heart of any organisation being able to retain its talent. He identifies four dimensions of emotional intelligence.

1. *Self-awareness:* a deep understanding of one's strengths and limitations, emotions, and the way we come across to others.
2. *Self-management:* a leader's emotions have public consequences and need to be managed.
3. *Social awareness:* this has to do with "reading" others, and knowing how to be empathetic.
4. *Relational management:* this boils down to handling other people's emotions, with the knack of finding common ground.

A leader's growth in these four dimensions cultivates an atmosphere where "resonance" prevails over "dissonance". This is

---

[130] Daniel Goleman, *The New Leaders* (London: Time Warner, 2003).

the glue that holds teams together. Resonance stems, not from a leader's good moods, but from a whole set of co-ordinated activities which includes choosing the right leadership style at any particular time.

The Leader and Vision

Seeing clearly

The essential meaning of vision is to see where one is going. So when Jesus warned his disciples about "blind guides" (Matthew 15:14) he was indicating that they were no use, even dangerous, because they had no vision and would lead others into a ditch. Words mean different things to different people. The word "vision" is no exception. I know of an outstanding church in a principal university city where the minister resolutely refused to speak in terms of "vision", believing that it would detract from a God-centred emphasis. In actual fact he was one of the most visionary leaders I have ever known. So although our use of language may differ, what is certain is that God himself is able to make vision clear.

God said through Isaiah, "Whether you turn to the right or to the left, your ears will hear a voice behind you saying, this is the way, walk in it" (Isaiah 30:21). Accordingly, we should have great confidence in God's ability to speak to us. The good news about Jesus is to be the foundation of every church's vision. This is where the leader must focus his thoughts and prayers.

For sure, no church is perfect, or will strike the right balance between form and freedom all the time. But despite the shortcomings, my testimony is one of huge thankfulness to God for the church, the local community of which I am a part, that teaches, challenges and encourages me as a follower of Jesus, along with other believers. Where else would I interact with such a variety of people through whom God confronts my selfishness and independence, and imparts so much into my life? Some may argue that without the church there may be less for the world to stumble over, but there would surely also be less of the visible Jesus to see? The best leaders of local churches will be those who are convinced that there is no higher privilege in the world than leading a church, and convinced that its reason for existence is found in the gospel.

Isaiah's calling reminds us that vision *of* God always precedes vision *from* God. Vision is deeply theological. What we are to see clearly is him. "I saw the Lord seated on a throne, high and exalted" (Isaiah 6:1). As a consequence of this encounter, every one of Isaiah's sixty-six chapters speaks about God. He is overcome by his kingship, sovereignty and holiness. It is all about God doing something for him. Grace always works this way: allowing God to serve us before we can serve him. God takes a live coal from the altar, touches Isaiah's lips and says, "Your guilt is taken away and your sin atoned for" (v.7). It is only after seeing God, and experiencing his grace, that the particulars of Isaiah's assignment are revealed: Who: "Go and tell this people" (v.9); What: the message he is to speak (v.9–10); and When: the time frame for his assignment (v.11–13). It is the encounter with God that gives passion and conviction to the task.

Communicating tangibly

Arguably, the easiest part of articulating vision is at the start of a newly planted church, or when a pastor starts a new tenure. Fresh energy and inspiration accompany that newness. Far more demanding, and of greater long-term significance, is the stewarding of vision over the years as a church develops. As

Leadership Culture

time passes, the leader will find it harder and harder to lead purely by innovation or human energy. The resources have to be found elsewhere.

It is not uncommon to hear the comment, "I don't know what the vision is". This is puzzling and somewhat galling to many good leaders, and the response is usually to take people back to the church's mission statement or strap line which expresses its purpose. But, to the leader's consternation, they shake their heads and say, "No, that's not it", or they simply look at him or her with dissatisfied unbelief on their face. What is going on in this conversation? Are these people slow to catch on? Or might they be telling us something important? At the very least, it reminds us that people crave a clearly articulated vision. It highlights the need to articulate the difference between our mission statement which stays largely the same (the biblical mandate), and vision which is distinct, even unique and evolving, for that church's time and setting.

People are looking for something that goes beyond a generic purpose, and which expresses specific detail about the church's calling and how it will make a difference where it is. Sometimes the impression is given that vision comes out of the blue with little or no accompanying effort and participation by us. More realistically, I think, is to see vision-building as an ongoing process. Vision is not static. It involves listening afresh to God and drawing other leaders in to that process. This is the only way to deepen a shared ownership of vision. As a result smaller "visions" within the overall vision are likely to emerge. Good leaders will find themselves enabling the sometimes "wild" ideas of others which fit the overall vision.

Visionary leaders paint a picture of what the future is going to look like. Whether it be Winston Churchill's wartime speeches, or Martin Luther-King's "I Have a Dream" speech, they all contrast the present with a better future. Vision is not just about downloading information; it turns ears into eyes so that we all see something of God's future. Vision must be communicated by the example of the leader's life. Our life is a message and we share and live what God has said and shown. We tell our own story of how God encountered us, our weakness but God's faithfulness. Leaders also let the church hear the story of others.

Renewing deeply

Experience tells us that leaders who commit to local church ministry for the long haul will, at various times, grow weary and be severely tested. These struggles are part of leadership. They seem to happen over and over when various props get knocked away. By God's grace we can come to see the removal of props as a gift to confront us in our disorientation. Seasons like these can be overwhelming and painful and, if left unattended, can lead to both the leader's stagnation and that of the church's ministry.

The danger at this time is like that of the boiled frog story. Because the water is heating up slowly the frog doesn't realize it is being cooked alive and fails to leap out of the pot. Likewise, times of struggle and disillusionment have the potential to lead to significant crisis. These struggles need to be addressed, and may require urgent action. Three responses are possible at this point. The first is to ignore what is going on (like the frog) and settle for a slow death. The second is to plan one's exit from ministry, believing that the circumstances are to blame. The third way, often excruciatingly painful and humbling, is to acknowledge that I have a choice, and that I desperately need

God's help and that of others.

Like Isaiah, our greatest need is not for a new strategy, but to see God; to meet him and to hear from Him. In that encounter we learn afresh about God's love and power, as well as learning new things about ourselves. We discover the issues have far more to do with our heart and thinking, than they do with our circumstances. Some years ago, a combination of personal losses and poorly managed ministry stress, led to such a season in my life. One of the things that helped me, while on sabbatical, was coming to see that old patterns of stagnation could be broken. For me, it involved a new pattern of retreat and study. This allowed for another kind of learning, a learning that helped me to move from what I knew, and discover what I needed.

How we respond in these seasons of trial is crucial. They serve to focus us on what really matters in life and ministry. There are no shortcuts; making a trade-off of some kind will not get us to God or effect real change. It is time to find out again, as one friend expressed it, what God wants you to do, and then to do it with all your heart.

Once that sense of personal direction from God begins to be renewed, we are able to re-engage fully with the church's vision. Remind yourself that God allows these seasons so that he can demonstrate, through our weakness, his unmistakable grace and power. He loves us and wants peace and trust to reign in our hearts. This is why he gives us things to do which only he can accomplish. We need not fear that our egos will run away with us. God has his way of keeping us exactly where he wants us, even when we are stewarding a large vision. So, from time to time, we will be criticized unjustly (and sometimes justly!), we will make stupid mistakes and problems will occur that can only be solved by prayer. God uses them all.

We are told that leadership is about influence. This is true. However, Jesus spoke in terms of serving others, and placed an emphasis upon our relationships. Influence happens in many ways, but most powerfully through the leader's servanthood. This is the kingdom at work. It is this relationship component of leadership through which vision is most powerfully imparted.

CHAPTER 10

Churches that Develop Leaders

The development of leaders is one of those activities, which, if done with dedication, will really make a difference. There are many things for a leader to do. But the key to greater fruitfulness is often doing less, not more. It is concentrating on the activities that really count.

In horticulture the point of pruning is to enable the plant to do less so that it can concentrate its resource and energy on producing fruit. Some activities have to go, but developing leaders must not be one of them. I have found it true over the years that if God really wants us to develop leaders he will give us what we need to get started.

The Limiting Factor

The fruitfulness of church ministry is always, to some extent, limited by the number of available leaders. Demand seems to exceed supply. Or as Jesus said, "The harvest is plentiful but the workers are few" (Matthew 9:37).

Uncomfortable Growth

The answer that the Bible robustly holds forth, in both Old and New Testaments, is for leaders to understand their role in training and multiplying further leadership. Jethro's counsel to Moses is timeless wisdom and pretty blunt! "What you are doing is not good. You and these people who come to you will only wear yourselves out. The work is too heavy for you; you cannot handle it alone" (Exodus 18:17–18). Leadership should always involve more than one.

Moses, as the lead leader, has his God-given responsibilities: to teach and show the people how to live, and to select and appoint leaders to share the load. This selection is on the basis of their gifting and capacity (Exodus 18:19–23). For me, the significance of this counsel never fails to be highlighted by the following simple and familiar diagram (Figure 9).

Figure 9. Pyramid Principle

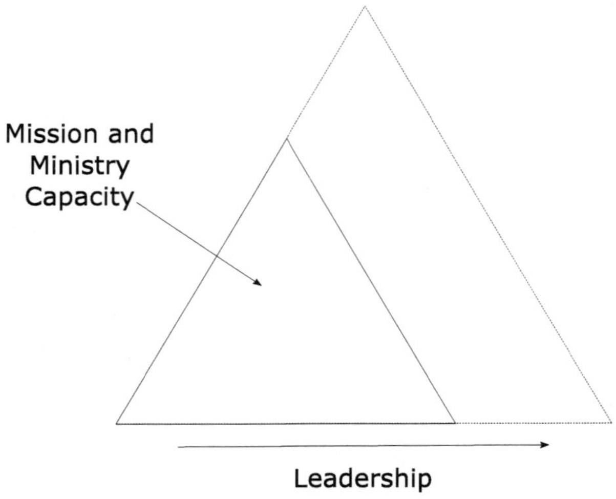

Known as the pyramid principle, where the base determines the height, the addition of leadership along the base expands the capacity for overall mission and ministry (the volume of the pyramid).

In the New Testament, we see Jesus doing exactly this. As the days went on, he gave more and more of his time to training the twelve. His intention was to leave behind a small group of leaders to continue his ministry. Later on Paul underlines the same priority, namely that those with principal leadership gifts are to use them to develop others, "to prepare God's people for works of service" (Ephesians 4:12). Therefore, leaders who simply exercise their gifts for ministry, and yet neglect to train others, will seriously limit their fruitfulness. It has been said that when leaders stand before God he will not so much be interested in asking what they have done for him, but what they have helped others do for him.

However leadership development rarely seems to attract sufficient time and effort from leaders today. Maybe Moses' slowness to grasp this principle, along with our own, is symptomatic of a wider human tendency? At the time of the Reformation, an understanding was clearly gained of the priesthood of all believers. But what was gained theologically did not fully translate into practice. The priest moved from the altar to the pulpit, but ministry largely remained in the hands of the clergy.

The authors of *The Leadership Pipeline* underline this same issue within secular organisations.[131] Their solution is to create a leadership development process that functions like a pipeline in producing a continual flow of leaders. We can learn from

---

[131] Ram Charan, Stephen Drotter and James Noel, *The Leadership Pipeline: How To Build The Leadership-Powered Company* (San Francisco: Jossey-Bass, 2001), 1.

Experience indicates that many kinds ... the pipeline but this should not deter ...loping leaders.

...rs

...t training and empowering disciples. In ...ellent book, *The Master Plan of Evangelism,* he identifies eight components that make up Jesus' strategy of making disciples and leaders: selection, association, consecration, impartation, demonstration, delegation, supervision and reproduction.[132] The question for the church in the twenty-first century, as in any age, is: Are our efforts faithfully reproducing Jesus' mission? Coleman's conclusion is, "There is but one hope to stem the tide: that is, a return on the part of the church to the Master's plan of evangelism."[133]

In the Vineyard, we have used a similar training process, known rather unimaginatively it has to be said, as IRTDMNR (Identify, Recruit, Train, Deploy, Monitor, Nurture, Reproduce). These are the vital activities we see in Jesus as he equips leaders.

1. We *identify* leaders by noticing, first of all, those who are naturally leading. Who do people listen to, talk about, and gravitate towards? We build genuine relationship with them. We don't need to hurry, because time is on our side. We want to learn about their character, capacity, chemistry with us, and their competence.
2. *Recruitment.* Jesus told his disciples to pray for workers

[132] Robert E. Colman, *The Master Plan of Evangelism* (Grand Rapids, MI: Fleming H. Revell, 1993).
[133] Ibid., 190.

for the harvest. Workers are needed, and some workers develop into leaders. Jesus was interested in choosing those whom his Father was calling. This is why he prayed and was able to say, "You did not choose me, but I chose you and appointed you to go and bear fruit" (John 15:16). Our job is not to motivate people, but to discover those who God has motivated.

3. Jesus' *training* of leaders followed the same pattern as his disciple-making. We are not to confuse information with training. Jesus disciples were trained on-the-job by being with him and watching him.
4. Following on-the-job training, new leaders are *deployed* to carry out specific ministry tasks. The new responsibilities must be clear, the expectations plain, and the training appropriate to the task.
5. *Monitoring* underlines the need for newly deployed leaders to have consistent ongoing relationship and contact with the coaching or overseeing leader. These times involved ongoing learning, feedback and problem solving.
6. *Nurturing* leaders requires listening and responding with counsel, encouragement and prayer.
7. *Reproduce.* Jesus showed his disciples how to develop this same life pattern in others so that leaders could be multiplied. The training we have received, we pass on to others.

Any training process runs the risk of being perceived as a cookie-cutter factory. Will we produce leaders who are all the same, or can individuality be expressed? Studies seem to show that effective leaders actually have little in common.[134] They differ in sex, age and race. They employ different styles that have different goals. Yet despite their differences, they share one common trait: they do not hesitate to break virtually every rule.

Leading like Jesus, as we saw in the last chapter, is not about following a rule book which will dismiss thoughts of any new precedent. Sometimes a new precedent is exactly what *is* needed. Instead, the priority will be to identify with the Spirit of Jesus, and discover that it is sometimes the breaking of rules (doing the unexpected) that releases the power of the kingdom. If every person is different it makes sense to take that into account. As Buckingham and Coffman say, "I'm going to be very consistent with every one of you because I will treat every one of you differently."[135]

Mobilising a Leader-Developing Church

Use different sized groups

Jesus mobilised groups of varying sizes. The seventy-two had received some training before being sent on mission. The twelve disciples who formed a core group were intensively trained by Jesus over a number of years. Within that group there were three, Peter, James and John, with whom Jesus had a particularly close relationship, and who would have significant leadership responsibilities in the future. Although the numbers 3, 12 and 72 may seem biblically contrived, they do provide an understanding of the benefit of working with different sized groups.

---

[134]Marcus Buckingham and Curt Coffman, *First Break All The Rules: What the World's Greatest Managers Do Differently* (London: Pocket Books, 2005).
[135]Ibid., 156.

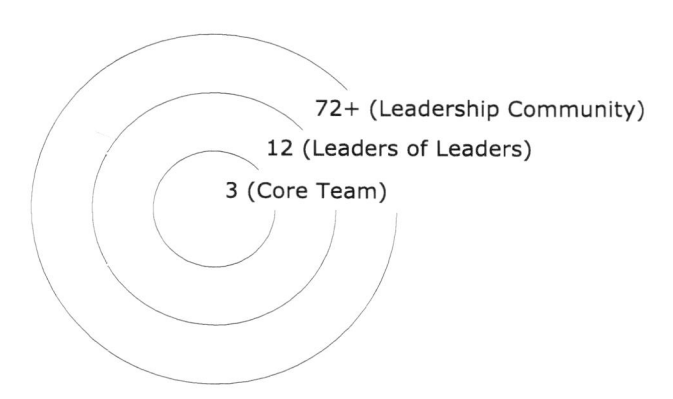

Figure 10. Training Leaders 3, 12, 72.

72+ (Leadership Community)
12 (Leaders of Leaders)
3 (Core Team)

In a local church setting Figure 10 represent the church's leadership. The larger group (72+) represents the entire church's leadership community (whatever its size), which gathers maybe three or four times a year. Three elements are typically part of these meetings. First, vision casting with the sharing of good news, stories, or short interviews, which make vision and values concrete. This cultivates ownership across the leadership community and regularly updates everyone on progress and needs. Secondly, a time devoted to teaching, training or development of some leadership skill. This is best done by allowing current needs to determine the training agenda. What skill needs to be affirmed and applied? It may be further training in the use of the Bible, or giving tips on building teams, applicable to all leaders. The third element can involve break-out groups, possibly ministry specific, to work on some aspect of planning or problem-solving. These times will be set in a context of worship, listening to what the Holy Spirit is saying, and time for prayer for one another.

The intermediate sized group of leaders (12) carries greater responsibility, overseeing and equipping other leaders in the church. These are the leaders of leaders, and ongoing training and interaction with these leaders will require a closer relational element. This is the size of group that we have already noted in detail when discussing disciple-making in in Chapter 7.

The smallest grouping (3) represents those individuals who have been selected and are the senior leadership team of the church. This group will be collegiate in nature, and must be given priority and opportunity for ongoing growth, learning and responsibility. Or it may be that this sized grouping represents the leader's coaching commitments – three young leaders who he or she is developing.

These different groupings create a leadership culture within the church. This culture is further strengthened by holding regular leadership orientation seminars, an introductory teaching open to all, covering leadership values and vision. It is a helpful means of identifying new potential leaders for further training and involvement.

Multiply leaders through small groups

Small groups provide a vital building block for developing a healthy church. These groups become more essential as a church grows larger, providing a place for pastoral care and ongoing discipling. Small groups are like the church in microcosm and therefore provide an excellent place for leaders to be trained and gain experience.

A way to mobilise small group leadership is shown below. Described here as a *leaders apprenticeship group* (LAG) it can, of course, be tweaked to suit different church contexts. Fig 11 illustrates the process.

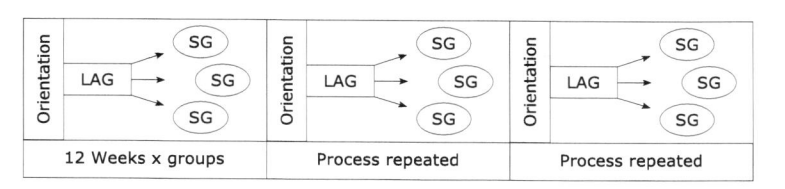

Figure 11. Leadership Apprentice Group Process

Orientation — LAG → SG, SG, SG	Orientation — LAG → SG, SG, SG	Orientation — LAG → SG, SG, SG
12 Weeks x groups	Process repeated	Process repeated

The process starts with an orientation training/welcome for newcomers to the church that, typically, explains the essence of Christianity, together with the vision and values and how people can become meaningfully involved. The participants in the orientation are invited, as a next step, to join a group (LAG) which contains a number of apprentice leaders besides the main leader. The trainer models leadership appropriate to the group. He or she also provides the apprentice leaders with hands-on experience and gives regular feedback.

A *leaders apprenticeship group* runs, say, for twelve weeks, with the dual purpose of training new leaders, and integrating newcomers into the life of the church. After that time, and on the basis of formed relationships, the apprentice leaders are released with a small number of new people in order to grow and reproduce their own small group (SG). The whole process can be repeated at regular intervals and contributes toward developing a regular supply of new leaders and new small groups.

One Church's Experience: Developing Leaders at Riverside Vineyard

From the start of RVC, Lulu and I assumed everyone was a potential leader until they proved otherwise! We expected everyone to participate. Giving the ministry back to the people had been drummed into us.

Over the years at RVC we have done different things with leaders at different times. Leadership development has no definitive, "one size fits all" programme but rather it requires the intentional application of good training practice. Consequently, at certain points in our church history we have led a variety of leadership development groups, from small groups in our own home, through to a two-year leadership development school.

The different formats depended on the current circumstances of those invited, and that of the church. These determined the most suitable means of training delivery. I share our experience of the leadership school, not because I believe it to be the most effective means of training, but because its components may be helpful in thinking through your own approach to developing leaders.

Leadership Development School

It seemed to us that there was no point in re-inventing the training wheel. When we designed our two-year leadership development school we looked carefully at a number of difference church approaches to training, including Evanston Vineyard and Vineyard Columbus. These churches, led by our friends Steve and Cindy Nicolson, and Rich and Marlene Nathan respectively, had strong track records in developing leaders, and we ourselves had benefited immensely from them. Drawing on their experience, while considering our own context, we came up with the following scheme for training:

Objectives

Our church's vision centred around planting and developing churches throughout the UK and beyond. The training of leaders therefore was of the highest priority to us. I wrote in the original brochure, "My passion is to bring together the thoughtful and careful use of God's word with the empowering of the Holy Spirit for life and ministry". The school was rather grandly called, "The Vineyard School for Church Leadership and Biblical Studies", which was nevertheless an accurate description of what we were trying to accomplish.

The goal was to develop people who were biblically and theologically proficient, aware of personal strengths and areas for growth, able to minister effectively, and confident in God's call, gifting and direction for their lives. Further priorities included a close devotion to God, growing maturity, and love for the church and church planting as a means of extending God's kingdom.

Our approach to training

Training in a church-based context has various advantages. For many, bible college is difficult to attend for financial and practical reasons. Church-based training keeps people connected with the church, ministry opportunities and existing relationships. The elements of hands-on ministry experience and personal interaction with leaders, elements so clearly seen in the ministry of Jesus, were to be a principal feature.

The approach was an integration of biblical studies, leadership skills, and hands-on ministry experience, held together by a coaching dimension. I pictured it as two lines of a railway track (biblical studies and leadership skills), laid upon a foundation of spiritual formation, and heading towards the specific objective of all round leadership development.

Time commitment

It was a two-year programme, consisting of six terms, each of ten weeks duration. During term-time there was a weekly midweek evening, alternating biblical studies and leadership skills input. There was also a Saturday intensive teaching each term. Every student was assigned to a group (no more than eight people) led by a coach. These groups met every other week for interaction during the second half of the leadership skills evening.

In addition, the coach would have two one-on-one sessions with individuals each term. Trainees required time for reading, self-study and agreed/assigned practical ministry in and through the church. Each year there was a residential weekend away as well as involvement in ministry trips to other churches.

Training components

The four components we used are shown in Figure 12.

Figure 12. Effective Training Components

- Biblical Studies
- Spiritual and Leadership Formation
- Hands on Experience
- **Coaching**

Biblical studies

Growing in biblical understanding and theological awareness is vital for any leader. A leader's specific call, purpose and contribution will largely be derived biblically, and their own development and maturity will be based on their growing understanding and application of God's word. The teaching of God's word happens in many different settings and contexts, and all leaders, no matter what their area of contribution, will benefit from growing in their ability to share God's word with others, and particularly in one-on-one informal settings. The biblical studies syllabus consisted of the following: biblical foundations (Old and New Testament overviews and Bible interpretation); the Pentateuch; the Gospels; the kingdom in Scripture and theology; Paul's Letters; and the Acts of the Apostles. The Saturday intensives covered the Wisdom Literature (Dr. Don Williams) and the Holy Spirit in the Old and New Testament (Dr. Max Turner). Each term there was a set book.

Spiritual and leadership formation

Growing in Christlike character, as well as developing practical leadership habits, are indispensible. The leadership curriculum taught on areas such as a deepening devotional life, exploring the gifts that God has given, character and heart issues, and leadership and people skills. Other topics were covered such as getting a disciplined control over one's time, learning to plan, habits that promote personal development, which included regular reading and listening to good teaching, understanding conflict, growing in holiness, overcoming discouragement and so on.

Staff members taught the termly courses on leadership skills, with visiting speakers for the intensives, forums and weekends away.

Hands-on experience

Experience in all the different aspects of a church's ministry is valuable. Those areas of ministry that each person needed to experience were identified, taking into account their gift mix. Supervision was provided and on-going assessment of progress was discussed one-on-one at the end of each term.

We recognize that the leading of small groups forms one of the most valuable leadership development experiences, and attendees were encouraged to lead a small group where possible. A group provides experience in pastoring, teaching, planning, discipling, evangelizing and reproducing the group.

Coaching

The coaching element introduces a strong relational component and draws together the other elements. It greatly increases the effectiveness of the training. Coaching isn't about providing good answers; it is the art of asking good questions.[136] The best thing a coach can do for another person is to come alongside them and help them to think, and to listen to God for themselves. These are times to explore fundamental questions: What is it that you are trying to accomplish that will make a lasting difference? What are your particular struggles, and how are you responding to them? It is in these times of coaching and of prayer together that significant personal change can happen.

Critique of the School

The experience of running the two-year church-based school was effective at a number of levels but not sustainable in a rolling capacity for a church of our size. The benefits were worthwhile and significant, for both the trainees released more firmly into ministry and for the experience gained by teachers and coaches. The four interacting components of the training model provided an effective combination for church-based training, although inevitably some trainees felt themselves overstretched with the time commitment required.

Training developments in our movement, both nationally and internationally, mean that training resources can now more effectively be pooled and drawn upon, thereby taking the pressure off individual churches. Nationally, the creation of training hubs enables potential leaders from a number of churches in a

---

[136] Excellent coaching and practical leadership tools are available online from Dr. R.E. Logan, Coachnet, http://www.coachnet.org.

geographical area to gather regularly for training. Biblical and theological input as well as practical leadership courses at these centres come from highly experienced teachers and leaders.

As in other church networks, the Vineyard Institute, under the direction of Dr. Derek Morphew, functions as an umbrella theological provider with learning communities that can be customized to the needs and goals of both hubs and local churches.[137] However, for training to be effective, pastors of local churches must remain intentionally engaged in developing leaders through providing hands-on ministry experience and coaching.

To Sum Up

Growing churches will give priority to developing leaders so that the discipling and equipping of more people can proceed. There is no one programme or definitive way by which a church does this. Far more important is applying the practices for developing leaders that we see in the life of Jesus. God's word must be allowed to inform and form the leader. This happens as that person serves others, learning through experience, and with the help and coaching of seasoned leaders.

Discussion Questions on Leadership

1. "We influence others through vision and organisation, but the most significant influence of leadership flows through values and relationship." How does this statement compare with what Jesus said in Mark 10:35–45? At which point on Figure 8 do you think your leadership operates? Do others

---

[137]Vineyard Institute, http://vineyardinstitute.org.

agree? How might Jesus' way of leading be strengthened in your life and church?
2. For study: Isaiah 6:1–13. Is your vision inspired and developed from this same source? What is God specifically calling you and your church to do that will make a lasting difference? What particular things has God allowed you and your church to do with excellence, that he is blessing?
3. Figure 9 reminds us that the quantity and quality of leaders is a limiting factor of ongoing health and growth in the church. Although there is no one way to develop leaders, what is your agreed and intentional plan to do this? How can this activity be given the necessary time, energy and resource? Do the training components in Figure 12 assist in designing an approach that is do-able?

Recommended Books on Leadership

1. Chris Lowney, *Heroic Leadership: Best Practices from a 450-Year-Old Company that Changed the World* (Chicago: Loyola Press, 2003). The story of the Jesuits is told in inspiring and practical terms.
2. Walter C. Wright, *Relational Leadership: A Biblical Model for Influence and Service* (Downers Grove, IL, 2009). Presents an in-depth case for relational leadership.
3. Daniel Goleman, *The New Leaders* (London: Time Warner, 2003). Explains how resonance is created through the leader's growth in emotional intelligence.

CHAPTER 11

Planting Churches

An Inspiring Example: A Church that Gives Birth

Churches have the inbuilt potential to reproduce and multiply. It was this concept, as a new church planter, that captured my imagination. If God enabled churches to reproduce, might it not be possible for significant missional impact to come from something that begins so small and weak? I remember at the time being deeply struck by a church planting story.

It was the story of a funeral with a difference. In fact there were two unusual things about the funeral. The first was that the deceased was a church, and the second, that the funeral was very large. The church whose funeral it was, largely made up of Puerto Rican origin, had over the course of its life planted out fifty-six churches and now, having run its course, was being laid to rest. So people from the fifty-six church plants returned over the course of a weekend, in groups of up to one thousand at a time, to give thanks to God for the life they had been given through this mother church. The story had such a ring of the kingdom about it: fruitful multiplication, sacrificial self-giving, joy and sorrow. Someone once said that the world is constantly changed by committed minorities and not by apathetic majorities. Here was a church community seeking to live that out in its own way.

The Miracle of Multiplication

In the Museum of Science and Industry in Chicago there is a simple display illustrating the power of multiplication. A chequerboard 8x8 has one grain of rice placed on the first square, two grains of rice on the second square, four on the third, eight on the fourth, sixteen on the fifth and so on. The question is then posed, "At this rate of multiplication, how much rice would there be on the chequerboard by the time the last square was reached (the 64th square)? The answer is given by pressing a button on a console. Enough rice to cover the entire subcontinent of India fifty feet deep, 153 billion tonnes of rice, which is evidently more than the world's rice harvest for the next one thousand years! The power of multiplication stretches our thinking.

Neil Cole uses this illustration to highlight the dramatic difference between addition and multiplication in church ministry.[138] The tendency is to think in terms of addition: adding one more person to a team, adding one more small group and so on. However, for example, equipping *all* small group leaders to *each* grow and multiply their small group would rapidly increase growth. Nevertheless, multiplication requires more intentional effort by all to achieve. It feels more costly than addition especially in the early stages – more costly in time,

---

[138]Cole, *Cultivating A Life For God*, 22–25.

more costly in training and more costly in relationships. However, if the multiplication approach is maintained over time it will of course far outstrip the addition approach.

It is a stirring thought for those who are serious about the Great Commission. The population of the world is multiplying while much of the Western church is shrinking or at best, engaged in addition. This is why the dynamics of church planting can be of relevance to every church.

Jesus' parables, which explain what the kingdom of God is like, often point to its propensity to grow and multiply from the smallest beginnings. The parable of the growing seed (Mark 4:26–29) speaks of the seed's innate ability to multiply itself. In fact, we are specifically told the seed grows irrespective of what the farmer does (sleeping or getting up). At the same time the parable reminds us that the seeds do not grow endlessly in size, but instead reproduce themselves, "first the stalk, then the head, then the full kernel in the head" (v.28). When the seed is ripe it is ready for harvest (v.29). The reproduction and multiplication of churches, whereby a church gives birth to new churches that in turn birth more churches is the essence of a church planting vision.

The Church Planting Goal

Church multiplication is not simply about planting a church, or even several churches, but having a goal to plant "planting" churches. This requires the transmission of a multiplication conviction from church generation to generation. Robert Logan and Neil Cole, in their book, *Beyond Church Planting,* express this generational challenge by speaking of the need to "multiply churches to the third and fourth generation before claiming you have multiplied your church".[139]

It is one thing to believe, in some theoretical sense that the church is intended to grow and multiply. It is quite another to give priority to imparting that principle. It needs to become part of a church's spiritual DNA. Nor can it simply be one-dimensional: such as dreaming about planting a church but without the practice of multiplying disciples, multiplying small groups, multiplying leaders, and seeking to multiply every aspect of ministry in and through the church. I well remember at our commissioning service, prior to being sent out to plant, hearing that the vast majority of churches that had been planted in our movement had come from a relatively small number of churches. I was astounded. I naively thought that in a church planting movement that was what every church did. My prayer during that service was that God might allow us to be one of those churches that planted other planting churches.

As the days and years went by, God provided sufficient challenges to humble my perspective, but also sufficient encouragements to keep us pressing on. In times of hardship and struggle, we inevitably wonder whether our efforts to multiply ministry are worthwhile. At such times, I have frequently gained encouragement from C.H. Spurgeon. Late one afternoon, while out walking with a friend in nineteenth century London, they watched, up ahead of them, a man lighting gas street lamps. When he disappeared over the brow of a hill, Spurgeon turned to his companion and said that that was exactly what he wanted his life to be like. Like a lamp-lighter,

---

[139]Robert E. Logan and Neil Cole, *Beyond Church Planting: Pathways For Emerging Churches: Knowing God, Loving Others, Growing The Kingdom* (Carol Stream, IL: ChurchSmart Resources, 2005), 114.

who leaves behind a great deal that has been set alight. What might God allow us to leave behind if we embrace multiplication and planting into our lives?

Churches find themselves in different contexts, streams and denominations, where opportunities vary. How then, in each setting, might this principle of multiplication be applied? There are many ways. Some will focus on the training and resourcing of leaders and future ministers. Others will multiply services on Sunday or during the week, or multiply congregations through mission outposts or a campus/satellite model. Involvement in world mission, or partnering with church planting movements in other parts of the world, are further opportunities. Or it may be that we work together with other churches to plant a new church together, each providing different resources. Every church can find ways to contribute to the multiplication of ministry.

Life Out of Death

Not for a moment should we be carried away by a triumphalist spirit. All church planting practitioners wish that church multiplication were as easy as adding yeast to dough. In reality, multiplication growth is uncomfortable and requires challenging and costly effort to find the right ingredients for one's setting. It is far from easy.

In the prelude to his final Passover recorded in John's Gospel, we find these words embedded in Jesus' prediction of his coming death and resurrection: "I tell you the truth, unless a grain of wheat falls to the ground and dies, it remains only a single seed. But if it dies it produces many seeds" (John 12:24). Before Jesus' prediction, there had been the climactic sign of the raising of Lazarus (John 11:1–44). As a result many believed (v.45), but the Sanhedrin plotted to destroy Jesus, with the High Priest unwittingly prophesying that one man (Jesus) would die for both the Jewish nation and all the "scattered children of God" (John 11:51,52). The seed analogy, which Jesus used to describe the conclusion of his earthly mission, resonates with church planting application.

Church planting also involves a dying and a rising. In the very next verse, Jesus goes on to say, "The man who loves his life will lose it, while the man who hates his life in this world will keep it for eternal life. Whoever serves me must follow me; and where I am, my servant also will be" (John 12:25,26). Nothing short of the death of a seed will enable the re-creation of further seeds. Church planting is the creation of new communities of Christian faith, rising out of the planting of kingdom seed in every geographic and cultural context.

Planting involves movement, deep change and new life. First, it involves *movement*, in that seed is taken from one place and planted in the soil of a new environment or community. In practice, this often means moving to a new community and starting from scratch. Secondly, planting is an invitation for *deep change*, to "come and die", to echo Bonhoeffer's words. In the new location the seed dies to its original life as it commits to its new setting, and in God's time rises to become something different from what it was before. A church plant can never be the clone of the sending church (although many try) but rather has to find the fresh expression and resurrected shape of its life in the new community. Thirdly, and this is what sustains the church planting experience, is God's promise of *new life*. What was single (the seed) can become many (multiple seeds). Nothing in this planting picture is anything but costly and supernaturally miraculous.

Creating a Church Planting Culture

Only by total commitment will a church planting ethos be seeded in a local church. The extent of the task will soon become apparent to the leaders and people as they feel the pull of familiarity and self-preservation. A number of factors will, therefore, be necessary:

1. The pastor will need to settle the church planting issue in his or her own heart and mind. Is church planting a non-negotiable part of the vision for the church? If it is, integrate church planting into the church's vision from day one.
2. The leaders lead the way in praying for the release of church planting, and for called, God-given church planters. What do you collectively believe God wants you to accomplish in church planting over the next 5–10 years?
3. Share regularly with the whole church the church planting vision. This will include teaching and creating opportunities that awaken a sense of adventure and risk-taking. Deliberately undermine the culture's obsession with "safety". Challenge the whole church about the cost they are prepared to pay in order to see church planting happen.
4. Have an intentional means of spending time with, and training potential leaders and church planters. Test their sense of calling through faithful service and ministry experience. Talk about the future and clarify expectations. Ask the Holy Spirit to speak, guide and empower.
5. Insist on deep discipleship.
6. Demonstrate multiplication of ministry at every level of church life.

7. Draw inspiration and encouragement from the wider movement. Connect with other pastors who are passionate about reproducing churches, and have potential church planters rub shoulders with others on the same journey.

Next generation leaders

One of the greatest injustices we do to our young people is to ask them to be conservative. So said Francis Schaeffer, in his book, *The Church at the End of the Twentieth Century*.[140] It would seem that the early church was largely a young people's movement. Most people didn't live very long anyway – average life expectancy was no more than forty-five years. A commitment to the next generation of leaders does not deny the necessary contribution of older, seasoned leaders. Rather, it is the recognition that experience needs to be gained, and roles need to change. Therefore, our churches are to be clear about both the goal of raising up a new generation of leaders, and providing the opportunities for that to take place.

This commitment in local churches is not to be confused with a glorification of youth, but rather a kingdom principle of giving away to others (in this case, the next generation). Young leaders do not automatically know what they should be doing or have the maturity that many situations will demand. Seasoned leaders will in fact be needed more, to give time to being coaches and provide teaching, wise counsel and encouragement. With this kind of support, young leaders can flourish as they are resourced appropriately, trusted to experiment, and allowed to critique the way things are currently done in the church.

[140] Francis A. Schaeffer, *The Church at the End of the 20th Century* (Wheaton, IL: Crossway Books, 1985).

Roland Allen emphasised this need in his groundbreaking missional work, *A Spontaneous Expansion of the Church*.[141] Movements must loosen control and give liberty to those who are being developed for leadership. We need next generation leaders to experiment with different models of church planting; to take ownership of the biblical mandate to go into all the world, make disciples, and to keep growing in character and Christlikeness.

Church planting convictions

It begins with believing that the church, your church, has the seeds of self-propagation. That said, church planting is not an end in itself. The danger is that a mission strategy – in this instance church planting – may be confused with the necessary missional practices that underlie effective gospel kingdom mission. We should not assume that mission automatically takes place because there is a church plant. With this in mind, we are able to articulate and teach certain convictions and realities about church planting that strengthen its culture in the church. Such convictions include:

1. God alone is able to grow what has been planted and watered, "I planted the seed, Apollos watered it, but God made it grow" (1 Corinthians 3:6).
2. Planting new churches is one of the keys of fulfilling the Great Commission, as we saw in Chapter 6. The gospels, the book of Acts and the epistles can all be read as mission documents shedding light on how new com-

---

[141] Roland Allen, *The Spontaneous Expansion of the Church: And the Causes That Hinder It* (Eugene, OR: Wifp and Stock Publishers, 1997).

munities of believers are formed and grow through the words and works of Jesus.
3. It will take all kinds of churches to reach all kinds of people. This is because of both changes within culture as well as the diversity between cultures. While Jesus and the Scriptures remain unchanging, the church's job is to shape itself in line with that unchanging message in an ever-changing world.

Planting Questions and Methodologies

"Who?", "where?" and "how?" to plant are basic questions that churches need to consider.

"*Who* should plant?" This question will focus around calling, vision and leadership qualities. A church planting team is desirable, but experience proves that a great deal depends upon the principal leader. Pioneering, resilience and strong vision are all necessary. Fresh ground needs to explored, and then broken, with the focus on sowing lots of spiritual seed. Church planters need to be constantly engaging with their community, meeting people and beginning the process of gathering. There can be no expectation that people will automatically come to you or that missional practice can be delegated to others.

Don't be in a hurry to send people out to plant. Enthusiasm can easily override necessary preparation and planning. The best planters are those who have gained significant experience. However, for those with less experience, planting a satellite church closer to the sending church is worth exploring.

"*Where* should you plant?" Knowledge and experience of the location prior to planting is helpful, but it cannot predict with any certainty the fruitfulness of that particular "soil". I well

ting a university friend in Australia, the fifth gen-
of a large and successful vineyard in the Hunter
ood on a hilltop, he pointed out a small parcel
away on a gully slope. Unremarkable in appearance, the vines on that soil, he told me, consistently produced gold medal wines.

Another way to come at the question "where to plant" is to ask "who is the plant for?" and "who is to be the field?" "For we are God's fellow workers; you are God's field" (1 Corinthians 3:9). Is the plant aiming to reach a particular people group? Given the diversity of many urban areas, how will the plant in such an area reflect that diversity? What level of contact do the people of the area have with Christianity and the church? Is the plant located in a particular neighbourhood, or is it for a network of people connected through something other than geography, such as a non-English language gathering or a common interest? We will have a sense of call and love for those God is wanting us to reach.

"*How* should you plant?" What church planting approach is to be used? Different expressions are used to describe various means of church planting. One of these draws on horticultural practice, using the language of runners, grafts, transplants and seeds.

1. "Runners", as on a strawberry plant, extend from the parent taking root nearby and growing into a fresh plant. In time, the runner, the biological link, withers and the plant exists as its own entity. These church plants are within commuting distance, and there can be various levels of support from the mother church. This planting process can be repeated many times into other nearby areas.

2. "Transplants" follow the practice of a large garden plant, lifted and divided, with the smaller divisions re-planted into new locations where there is space to grow. This type of church planting can be used when a church has reached its growth ceiling, but wants to continue to grow. It is like a plant that has become pot-bound but is then divided and replanted.

These two means of church planting have their own unique challenges. The Aylesbury Vineyard, planted out by RVC in 1997, was planted as a "runner" plant. The planters, Mick and Lynn Elias, established three small groups in Aylesbury whilst remaining a part of the mother church. For over six years they commuted to RVC on Sundays, a round trip of 110 miles. Only after the establishment of those three initial groups were they released as an autonomous church plant.

The experience of Robin and Sarah Gardiner, who planted Reading Vineyard, was more akin to a "transplant", with a large number of people initially going from Riverside to join them. They will tell their story in the next chapter.

3. "Grafts" are another means of releasing new life. Here the method follows the practice of splicing a fresh shoot into another plant. In church growth terms this involves a leader and his or her team joining an existing church that may be floundering or even dying. This seems to be a far more common practice amongst traditional churches attempting to revive a declining, or near redundant, church. The Vineyard has little experience of this type of growth.

However, somewhat similar to this, is church adoption.

This happens when an independent (and not necessarily struggling) church wants to be included in a family of churches that can provide resource and spiritual vigour. This model has its challenges for both parties, including how to maintain the genetic code of the family of churches, realising that every "graft" brings with it its own history and values. Adoptions clearly do not have the same opportunity as planted churches to build on a common foundation. For this reason we have been careful, even cautious, about adoptions. But we believe that the whole church belongs to God, and he calls people as he wills.

4. "Seeding" is yet another way of multiplying churches. It can take place through a seed being airborne, blown on the wind, perhaps a long way from its original place of development. In church planting terms the church planting team will be planted into a new and often distant area where they settle, find new homes and schools for their children, and start new jobs.

   This has been the predominant way by which RVC has planted. This was largely to do with the time and circumstances when there were few Vineyard churches anywhere in the country, rather than due to a preferred means of planting.

   The emphasis was placed upon training and developing the church planting couple, ensuring they had a wide range of hands-on ministry and leadership practice, before they moved to a new area to plant. In almost half the cases the church planters were on RVC's pastoral staff team. I believe that it is the church planters' development and preparation which remain the primary factors in church planting success.

Planting Churches

In the last chapter, we look at what can be learnt from RVC's church planting experience, and offer some thoughts on the future growth of church planting through the Vineyard in the UK and Ireland. I do this with the intention and hope that principles may be seen which are beneficial to any church or network of churches engaged in mission or contemplating church planting.

CHAPTER 12

Church Planting Reflections

Although this final chapter contains my reflections from experiences of church planting within the Vineyard, I want to underline the intention of this book. The order of priorities is 1) Christ; 2) God's Church; 3) the Vineyard. The history of the Vineyard in the UK would be a very different book. This book is about mission and church planting for all churches, with Vineyard simply appearing as an example – illustrating, often through limitations, principles and lessons that may be helpful to others.

Church planting may not seem immediately relevant to some readers. I would, nevertheless, contend that it provides a focus, albeit a challenging one, for the church to find ways of reproducing its ministry. All Christians and churches need to find ways of God's life-giving seed falling into the ground and dying so that many seeds can grow.

Riverside Vineyard's Church Planting Experience

The church planters

For the Vineyard, church planting is our primary model of doing mission.

Over the years at RVC we have sought to keep that as the central goal. God has faithfully provided remarkable and courageous church planters who each have a unique story to tell. It is not possible here to hear from all of them, but I do wish to acknowledge and honour their contribution and journey: Rob and Sarah Gardiner (Reading), Mike and Maggie Pearson (Portsmouth & Southampton), Rob and Cathy Clarke (Bournemouth), Mick and Lynn Elias (Aylesbury), Rob and Heidi Versluys (Alexandra Palace), Erik and Rebecca Jespersen (Woking), Tim and Pippa Peppiatt (Cambridge), Nino and Becky Moscardini (Wokingham), John and Patsy Graham (Richmond & North London), Chris and Maggie Parsons (Bury St. Edmunds), Toby and Carol Foster (St. Andrews), Steve and Lucy Barclay (Lymington & Basingstoke), Richard and Diana Bramall (Chichester) and Hendrik and Leonie Hattingh (Yeovil).

Each has sought to follow the call of God, sacrificed much, and used their gifts rather than burying them in the ground. At times, they themselves may feel less than satisfied with the outcomes. However, assessing ministry "results" in the kingdom is altogether different from doing so in the world. In the kingdom, at the end of the day, the Master pays those who worked part of a day just as much as those who worked the whole day (Matthew 20:1–16). Only in the kingdom does this wonderfully happen. All are equally valued, even those who may feel they are at the back of the line, or have hit some major obstacle.

I have asked a few of our church planters to tell their story, and am grateful for their insights and honesty.

Rob and Sarah Gardiner, Reading Vineyard

Rob and Sarah Gardiner were our first church planters, and Rob tells their story:

> As a young man in Reading, recently married and settling in to a successful career as a lawyer, I received a prophecy through a visiting speaker, who had come to the local church we were attending. I was told that I was to be a "pastor" and a "teacher", and informed that I should not strive to make this happen, but seek to be approved of by the Lord and be faithful to Him. This was in 1986, and in the two to three years that followed, it became clear that we were to join the Vineyard, thereby entailing a move from Reading to Middlesex to be a part of Riverside Vineyard.
>
> The move involved laying down the offer of a partnership in a thriving Law Firm. However, we went to Riverside absolutely certain we were in the centre of God's will. I laid aside the desire to be a church planter in Reading, and I simply concentrated on being faithful to God in all things.
>
> We spent nearly four years at Riverside Vineyard. After some time, we began to sense from God that we were to go back to Reading, and shortly after that, Rick spoke to us about whether we would go back to Reading to plant a church. With the support of Rick and Lulu, and the unequivocal knowledge that this was indeed God's call, we sold up and moved back to Reading.
>
> This was Easter 1994. There were a number of Riverside Vineyard small groups meeting midweek in Reading, which

Church Planting Reflections

we simply took over. In hindsight this was the worst thing we could have done. We should have closed the groups and let everybody know we were starting a new group for a new Vineyard.

The beginning was rocky. There were some individuals who were uncertain about where their loyalties lay, and though we initially gathered successfully, we found that we had a big back door, as numerous folk returned to Riverside or left to join other local churches. This process took around two and a half years to complete. The loss of people during that time affected morale and momentum. The church went "public" in September 1996 with 40 adults and 23 children (63 people). Three years later we had grown through 100 in attendance.

There is a sense in which nothing can truly prepare one for the task of church planting because so much is learned through the process of the actual experience. We cannot anticipate our emotional responses to the different challenges that come our way, nor understand that unique sense of responsibility of pastoral leadership, prior to planting. However, we consider ourselves very privileged to have spent time with Rick and Lulu. They have always put in place, structures for the training and nurturing of leaders and potential church planters. They verbalized the vision to be a church from which others could be birthed from the first moment we met them. We were given many training opportunities including small group leadership training, children's ministry leadership experience, training courses and one-to-one type mentoring with the purpose of becoming a pastor/church planter. The range of developmental opportunities was extensive, and meant that we were able to meet people who were also preparing for further ministry.

Update: Reading Vineyard is now known as Network Vineyard and is exploring a campus model of development. They have also run a Hub centre for training church planters, out of which four churches have been planted.

Tim and Pippa Peppiatt, Cambridge Vineyard

Tim and Pippa Peppiatt's story is very different. Tim takes up the story:

> Pip and I always had mission/evangelism in our hearts and had explored other avenues including working abroad earlier on in our marriage. I completed training as a GP but deliberately did not join a partnership in order to be available for what the Lord had in mind, and to help at home with a young family while maintaining a good degree of involvement at our church, Riverside Vineyard.
>
> Pippa had been to bible school and done a diploma in ministry at Kensington Temple. I am the son of a pastor and had seen church leadership at first hand. During a five-year period at RVC with Rick and Lulu we increasingly felt called to church plant. We were in a training/mobilizing church and we were caught up with that vision. The equipping ministry at Riverside was excellent and anointed.
>
> As for ourselves, we had some students in our home group and enjoyed them. We looked into where, in England, there were some students, but no Vineyard. We discovered there were Vineyards in London and Oxford, but not in Cambridge. At about that time we had some folks over to dinner and happened to talk about Cambridge. Over the dinner I felt my heart stirred. Then for five nights consecutively the Lord woke me in the night and impressed on me to go to

Cambridge. I could not get back to sleep until I agreed.

Did Rick push us, or did we pull to get away from RVC? A bit of both! Rick had an important role in the whole thing. Firstly he had invited us to explore the idea of planting by inviting us to various leadership church planting training groups. We also joined the two-year Vineyard church planting training track. Rick challenged and tested our call and did not make things easy for us. We wanted to go sooner than Rick was prepared to let us go. Friends and family thought we were mad to do it by ourselves, being bi-vocational and with a young family. We had always hoped we could do it with a team, but it did not work out that way. Rick did not encourage us to recruit others from Riverside and we were not quite sure why.

About 2 years later, in 1998, we moved to Cambridge. I did some locum work for a while and then got a GP Partnership in a city centre practice. I got some funny looks at the interview when I said the reason we had come to Cambridge was to help start a church.

When we landed we had thought that we would not start a group for 3–6 months and just try to make friends and settle in. The church consisted of Pippa and I, our three kids and the next-door neighbour's cat. The cat soon left once I unpacked my water pistol … Within a few weeks, however, we had a number of enquiries about the church and suddenly we had a group on our hands!

The Lord graciously brought along a young man with a catalytic and evangelistic gift who helped us in the early stages. We supported him in outreach onto a local deprived estate, and a second small group started there. This resulted in some conversions. The church began to meet on a Sunday, after about a year in a local community centre annexed to the estate. After eighteen months the church had grown to about twenty-five.

Geographically, we felt quite isolated from family and friends. Our sending church leaders and Vineyard "overseers" were encouraging, through visits or telephone, but it was limited contact due to their own busy schedules and churches. Our greatest sources of support were our parents and wider family, and a couple of friends who could genuinely empathise because they had planted a church the year before us. About a year into the plant, we began to wobble. I was getting depressed and stressed by the load of a young family, full time GP job and church leadership – something had to change. We began to pray about what to do and felt, that for the sake of our family and health, I had to give up GP work or we had to hand over leading the church. We believe that family comes before ministry.

At this time little did we know that God was preparing Andy and Ruth Chamberlain to move to Cambridge. We handed over leadership to them in summer 2000 and decided it was best to leave Cambridge. It seems then, that we were meant to plant the church, and then hand it on. It was a costly experience, but we did it out of obedience and with heaven in mind.

Update: Tim and Pippa now live in the south of England where Tim works for a GP practice and they attend a local Vineyard. They are also involved in mission work in East Africa.

Church Planting Reflections

Chris and Maggie Parsons, West Suffolk Vineyard, Bury St. Edmunds

Chris and Maggie Parsons' experience was different again. Chris was ordained into the Anglican Church, in which they served for fifteen years, and Maggie is a qualified teacher. They already had extensive pastoral experience and training. A sense of calling to the Vineyard grew and in 1994 they joined the staff of Riverside Vineyard.

In Chris's words:

We had joined Riverside with a clear word in our hearts to support Rick and Lulu as they developed the church in Middlesex. After serving there for six years, first as an assistant pastor, and then as Rick's Associate for five years, and Maggie also working full-time on the staff for the last three years, we felt an increasing call to return to Suffolk and to plant a church in Bury St. Edmunds.

I had helped run the church planters training track at Riverside for three church planting couples, and had taught some of the early church planting sessions as well as attended seminars on church planting. Maggie had run Young Vineyard at Riverside and helped with the accounts and staff oversight. Between us we had worked in every area of the church's life. This helped to prepare us. We wrote our church planting plan and began to prepare to make the move to Suffolk.

Because of Chris's position on the staff team Rick felt it best to keep our move confidential for a period from the church. The staff was informed and the church was told three months before we left. We were dependent upon God prompting people to come and talk to us about their own feelings about church planting with us in the future. This he did! Two couples approached us, one before the announcement was made, and another couple on the day of the announcement.

Maggie continues:

> All through our six years at Riverside, Chris kept coming back to the idea of church planting. It was not that it was particularly "talked up" at Riverside – on the contrary, church plants seemed to just "happen" out of the general environment of the church. I was unsettled at the prospect! We were settled in a church we loved – our kids were happy and developing their own relationship with God – we had friends around us – and there was loads to do – why give it all up and go into uncertainty?
>
> It came to a crunch in 1999 when I asked God at the National Leaders Conference, "Why don't you speak to me any more?" Clear as a bell came back the reply: "I am speaking all the time, but you don't want to hear what I have to say!!" I was shattered, but knew exactly to what God was referring.
>
> So we left our rented house in London and moved to Suffolk. We waited until September 2000 to start the church, giving us about six months from Chris's arrival to settle into new secular employment and new relationships. Two couples from Riverside Vineyard, including a worship leader, joined us. Over the summer of 2000 we gathered another two couples and one other person – all people who had heard that we were going to start a church. At our first small group, very unexpectedly, we had twelve people.
>
> One year after the launch of that first small group, Chris

started being paid for two days work a week by the church and continued working full time in a secular job. After three years of this, and having dropped down to part-time employment, Chris felt we should give all our time to the growing church. This was probably too soon to make the jump financially, but it seemed the right thing to do. There were many "ups and downs" during those early years with various relational disappointments. Not always seeing all we wanted in the church could be frustrating. "Had we given up so much to create *this*?" was a common feeling during the difficult times. Nevertheless we managed to hold people together and hold on ourselves and began to see a growing and healthy church emerge.

Update: West Suffolk Vineyard has planted five churches, using a satellite-type model, where legal and financial matters were managed centrally. The churches have now become fully autonomous. It is a centre for training in the East Anglia region. Chris and Maggie handed over the leadership of the church in 2014 to Mark and Louise Williams.

The Sending Church

The experience of church planting from the sending church's perspective is a mix of joy and sadnesses. Joy to see the church giving birth, but sadness in saying goodbye to friends, and conscious that we should have done more by way of support.

Looking back, however, I realize that at the times of planting, there were so many other things going on at Riverside: developing multiple services, establishing new ministries for the community, and initiating our training school. When church planters went out, especially when they were staff members, we

Uncomfortable Growth

often felt as though we were hanging on by our fingertips. But we felt an urgency to establish new church plants. It is right that we plant churches today with greater support structures. That having been said, I still passionately believe that the principal key to church planting is identifying real pioneers, and preparing them in the home church as thoroughly as possible. I think we were always honest about the cost involved. I remember a conversation with one potential planter where I suggested that I thought we had something to learn from viniculture. When new vines are planted they are left largely unattended for the first couple of years in order to be "hardened" and get established. Quite understandably this conversation was not received with great enthusiasm!

It is natural for the mother church to be affected by giving birth. This was certainly our experience as can be seen from Figure 13

Figure 13. Riverside Vineyard's Church Planting History 1990–2013

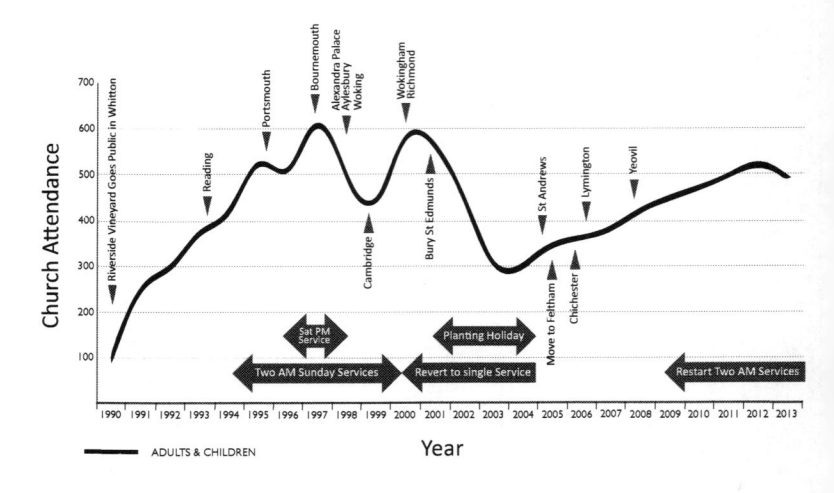

This graph shows the points in time (marked by vertical arrows) when churches were planted. This had a bearing upon the growth and attendance at Riverside. Decline in attendance and subsequent recovery growth followed the loss of seasoned leaders and/or pastors who had left with a church plant. This was particularly true in 1997 and 2000, when associate level pastors went out to plant. This calibre of leadership not only takes time to mature and replace, but remaining leadership has to find ways of filling the ministry gaps left behind. The upheaval that occurs is a good time to re-evaluate ministry priorities and possibly prune certain activities.

There is an emotional and spiritual dimension to church planting for the sending church. There were times, I think, when I overestimated the rate of church planting that Riverside could manage. So much so that by year 2000, having planted ten churches in seven years, we slumped into what I can only describe as a "planting fatigue". People were weary of saying goodbye. Attendance fell significantly. We needed time for recovery and I announced a "planting holiday" for a number of years. During this time no churches were planted and we spent time regrouping and growing as a church. Trial and error became the teacher for learning about the healthy rate and rhythm of church planting. As growth resumed at Riverside, so planting activity began again. Yes, it was uncomfortable growth.

During the "planting holiday" I spent considerable time thinking about our strategy and the future of the church. The so-called "regional church" model had served us well over the first ten years, with groups of people from quite far-flung areas (Reading, Aylesbury, North London) joining the church. However with the planting of churches into those areas, we no

Uncomfortable Growth

longer had people commuting from there. We were no longer "regional" in the same way, and saw this not as failure but as an aspect of vision having been fulfilled.

We began to look at, and invest more intentionally in, our local communities. We had run out of space in our rented facilities but were seemingly thwarted at every turn in acquiring our own church centre. With that prospect diminishing, I seriously wondered whether a multiple transplanting exercise might be the way forward, i.e. lifting and dividing the whole church into a number of different congregations/churches throughout our wider local area, each led by its own leaders.

On returning from sabbatical, still exhausted, we discovered that during our absence God had brought the possibility of acquiring an old printing factory site in Feltham. I thank God for our staff and leaders at that time who never gave up believing that God had a "home" for Riverside. Over the coming months and years the site in Feltham was purchased and redeveloped. It has provided a multiple-purpose, flexible facility for the ongoing vision and ministry of the church. Having our own church centre coincided with the increasing ethnic diversity of the church, which in itself was a stimulus to think and explore the possibilities of church planting contributions in other parts of the world. This is an exciting venture and, whilst still in its infancy, is brimming with potential and possibilities as we seek to partner with, and contribute towards, church planting movements in other countries.

Church Planting Reflections

The Church Planting Experience of Vineyard Churches UK and Ireland

The Vineyard's church planting history, since its beginnings in 1987, is depicted in Figure 14. The first five years were spent establishing the initial four church plants in order to have a platform from which to plant subsequent churches. Once the beachhead was established, church planting training became more intentional and, since 1992, the number of plants began to increase.

Figure 14. Vineyard Churches UK&I Church Planting History

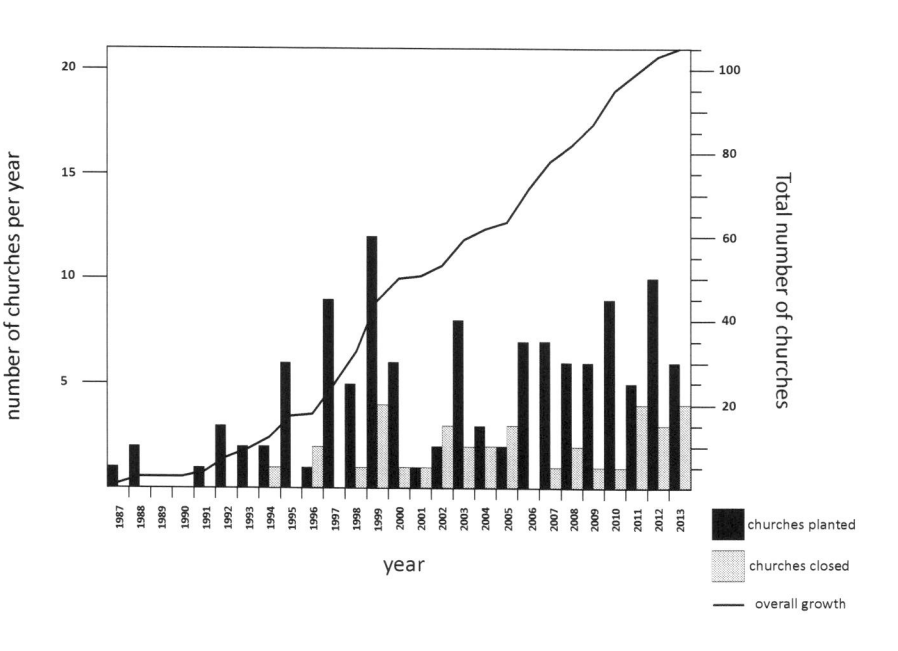

There is the old adage that says what gets measured gets done, and what gets done gets understood. Numbers are important and provide us with some objectivity. That having been said, I am not a statistician and will have to leave proper analysis to those qualified to do so. I can but make some general observations, maybe raising questions for further discussion.

1. The good news is that the graph shows that the Vineyard, as part of God's church in the UK, is growing. Churches continue to be planted and the cumulative number of churches is increasing.
2. We cannot tell from this graph what numbers of people are in the churches. By adding this metric, a fuller picture of growth and health could be seen. This is significant because growing churches are in a stronger position to plant churches.
3. Loss of churches through closures is in the 25–30% range of planted churches. This underlines the pioneering and risk-taking nature of our church planting model, and the need for viable support which does not quench the pioneering dynamic.
4. The rate of church planting from year to year is fairly consistent but with little net increase in relation to our growing number of churches.
5. The particular challenge is to go on exploring how to increase this rate of church planting.

These are challenging but I think legitimate issues to consider, and there has been no shortage of effort and heart searching expended on finding solutions. Anyone involved in church planting, indeed church leadership generally, is acutely aware that any kind of growth is God's doing. "So neither he who plants, nor he who waters is anything, but only God, who makes things grow" (1 Corinthians 3:7).

The approach of Natural Church Development is enormously helpful.[142] Commonly applied to analyzing the health of an individual church, it also has a significant application for movements and denominations. Extensive research from around the world has identified eight common "quality factors" that lead to a church's health. Its simple genius is twofold. First, is the willingness to tackle weaknesses and not simply focus on strengths, realizing that some weaknesses in the church (referred to as "minimum factors") can be like a hole below the water line, seriously affecting progress and wellbeing. Secondly, and this is crucial, is that feedback through a survey is obtained from a wide range of grassroots leaders (or pastors in a movement) so that an accurate picture is obtained of church or movement life. This reveals any blind spots. The "minimum factor" frequently turns out to be something unexpected. Actions can then be applied which will strengthen the areas of weakness and as a consequence lift overall fruitfulness.

The Dynamics of Movements

It is helpful to identify the contrasting characteristics of movements and institutions. This enables us to focus on developing a church culture and those activities, which enhance missional activity. "Churches with no movement dynamics are like a person on a life support machine".[143] These dynamics are vital for every church. It would, however, be simplistic to suggest that movements are always good, and institutions always bad.

---

[142]Natural Church Development, http://www.ncd-international.org/public/.
[143]Keller, *Center Church*, 337.

Organisations need elements of both in order to be dynamic as well as stable.

Furthermore "movement" dynamics can be strongly and helpfully evident in denominational churches, while "institutional" dynamics can creep up on movement churches. Keller contrasts institutional characteristics, such as top-down rules, regulations and procedures, with movement characteristics which are "flatter", less hierarchical and which stimulate new ideas, experimentation and develop new leaders.[144] The missional energy which every church wants is the dynamism which enables them to grow from within without needing to be propped up from outside.

David Garrison, in his book, *Church Planting Movements*, describes the emergence of church planting movements in a number of parts of the world.[145] He defines them as "a rapid and exponential increase of indigenous churches which plant churches within a given people group or population segment".[146] However, none of the movements cited by Garrison come from a Western context and the reasons for this are not altogether clear. Certainly there are significant contextual differences but we are still able to learn things from his observations.

Martin Robinson and Dwight Smith suggest that movements have four distinct phases.[147] First, there is the "divine spark" where an initial group of people are encountered by God. Second, is an "interpretive framework", where an explanation

---

[144]Ibid., 338–342.

[145]David Garrison, *Church Planting Movements: How God is Redeeming a Lost World* (Pasadena, CA: Mission Frontiers, 2000), 11–32.

[146]Ibid., 7.

[147]Martin Robinson and Dwight Smith, *Invading Secular Space: Strategies For Tomorrow's Church* (London: Monarch Books, 2003), 196.

Church Planting Reflections

of the spiritual encounter, with its implications, is provided. Third, there follows a "multiplication phase", where simple and replicable structures are developed. Fourth, a "permanence" or consolidation occurs through resourcing the mission. These four initial phases are illustrated in Figure 15.

Figure 15. Four Phases of a Movement

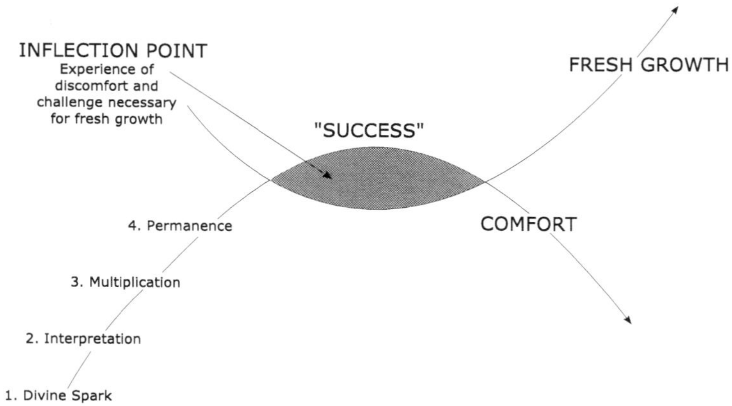

```
INFLECTION POINT                           FRESH GROWTH
Experience of
discomfort and
challenge necessary
for fresh growth          "SUCCESS"

                                           COMFORT
    4. Permanence

  3. Multiplication

2. Interpretation

1. Divine Spark
```

The initial energy or "divine spark" that birthed the Vineyard was, I believe, a sovereign and God-given impartation of his Spirit. Any church planting endeavour seems ridiculously audacious and requires determined action. Much of the "interpretation" of this divine spark had been brilliantly expounded and demonstrated by John Wimber and the Vineyard in North America. We knew that this impartation of the Spirit was to build the church and its evangelistic effectiveness. Priority was given to "multiplying" leaders and equipping church planters. As in nature, growth occurs in phases, and the first few years felt like an incubation period before significant growth. During this period, the culture of the movement was being established, providing a platform for growth and stability.

How Does a Movement Keep Growing?

Continuing growth in a church or network of churches is not automatic. Figure 15 (above) introduces diagrammatically the idea of a fresh wave of growth coming out of a new encounter with God, which is invariably challenging and uncomfortable (inflection point).

The Vineyard's journey in the UK and Ireland, together with its future opportunities, is depicted below in Figure 16. As recounted in Chapter 3, it began with a renewal phase, out of which a church planting phase was birthed. Phases 1 and 2 depict that journey. But what of future growth (phase 3)?

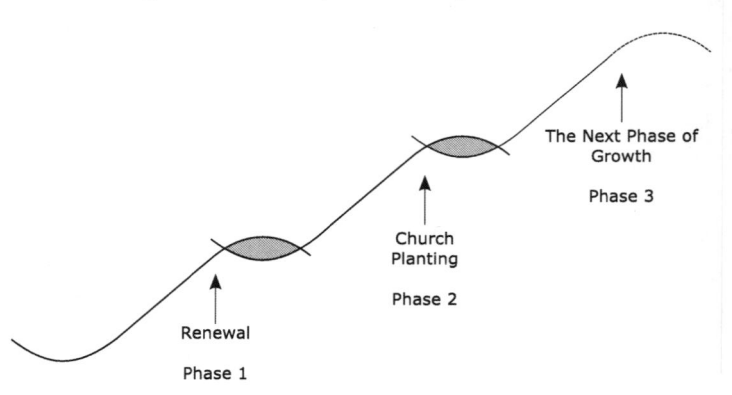

Figure 16. The Vineyard's Journey in the UK&I

Church Planting Reflections

Many are familiar with these 'S' shaped curves. In his book, *The Age of Paradox*[148], Charles Handy points to this curve as not only plotting the lifecycle of any organism, but also the life of an organisation, the progress of civilization and even the course of a relationship. Every new life or venture starts out falteringly at inception. It grows, enters a mature stage and finally begins to diminish and die. The opportunity during the mature stage is to see how another new life can begin (the start of a new S curve).

Where are we now on the curve? This is the question that any individual church or movement of churches will continually be asking. Is this a time for some godly realignment or new step of growth? Is this a tipping point for God to further release church planting? We know from experience that a new curve has an inception point (shaded area on the diagram); a time of discomfort, risk, faith and courage coming out of a fresh move of God's Spirit.

It is easy, looking back, to explain where we were on a curve, but difficult to see where we are now. All we know for sure is that we are in the gravest danger, ironically, when ministry and mission seem "successful" as we approach the top of a curve. Handy points us to the following considerations.

1. Always assume you are nearer the peak of the curve than you think. Nothing is lost by doing so, even if present growth goes on longer than expected. Useful preparatory work for the next curve will already have been done. More effort is required to turn the curve upwards again if it has already gone over the top.

---

[148]Charles B. Handy, *The Age of Paradox* (Watertown, MA: Harvard Business Review Press, 1995).

2. Whenever a new growth curve begins, the new and old curves co-exist for a time (shaded area). There is a need to sustain both curves during this transition period. The past and future co-exist in the present before the old gives way to the new.
3. Those who lead the new curve will probably not be those who led the last. However, the original leaders have a continuing responsibility to keep the first curve going long enough to support the early stages of the second one. Second curve leaders need to understand that much of what got them to where they are, are seldom the things to move them on. Work on the assumption that life will not continue as it was, and be willing to let go of the past.

These observations from Handy are undoubtedly worthy of study for the Vineyard or any growing church or movement. However we remind ourselves again that it is God who is at work. No amount of structural change in itself can accomplish God's growth and mission. Rather, at the centre of every new growth curve there must be something deeply of God, rather than man – some fresh impartation of his gospel, kingdom and Spirit. He alone is able to initiate the necessary spark to ignite all that is required for a fresh curve of growth. We know from Scripture that accompanying that divine initiative is the willingness of leaders to follow God's call. God uses people – often reluctant and inadequate – yet through them, a group or people emerge who are willing to give away all that God is giving.

To Sum Up

We know that living things neither grow endlessly in size, nor do they go on forever. They are birthed, grow, mature and maybe reproduce, before dying. Life continues by being passed on to others. This is true of the good news (we pass it on) and also of church communities who embody that good news. This huge privilege is passed on from one generation to another, and from one church to another.

As we give away, something miraculous happens. It is like the widow's meagre amount of flour and oil, given first to someone else (Elijah), leading to an endless supply of the very thing that was scarce. Fear, as Elijah pointed out to the widow, was the one thing that would prevent her from experiencing God's generous kindness (1 Kings 17:7–16). Fear makes us hold on to what we have. But every time we remember God's endless provision, and that he gives so that we may give away, we venture out again on that kingdom journey where the impossible becomes possible. It is precisely as we give and lose our life for Jesus and the sake of others that we find it has been saved (Luke 9:24). As Jim Elliott, missionary and martyr in South America, expressed so well, "He is no fool who gives what he cannot keep to gain what he cannot lose".[149]

Discussion Questions on Ministry Multiplication

1. Jesus' parables explaining the kingdom of God often point to the miracle of multiplication. For study: Mark 4:26–29. Identify from the parable the elements that are active in

---

[149]Elisabeth Elliott, *In the Shadow of the Almighty* (New York: Harper and Row, 1958), 108.

God's multiplication. How does each element relate to the ministry you want to see multiplied?
2. Figure 15 presents the development phases of a movement. It has been suggested that these "S" shaped curves can be applied to the development of individuals, ministries, churches and movements of churches. Choose an area of developmental application (e.g. your church or family of churches) and discuss where on the curve you think you are. Consider the points raised by Handy on p.209–210.
3. How could your church be engaged in some expression of church planting? Might the concepts of runners, grafts, transplants and seeds (discussed on p.186–188) provide a basis for thought? What might your church be able to contribute to a church plant?

Recommended Books on Planting and Developing Churches

1. Timothy Keller, *Center Church: Doing Balanced, gospel-Centered Ministry in Your City* (Grand Rapids, MI: Zondervan, 2012). A great overall resource on gospel theology, cultural engagement and movement dynamics.
2. Alan Hirsch, *The Forgotten Ways: Reactivating the Missional Church* (Grand Rapids: Brazos Press, 2006). Innovative thinking on disciple-making, community, church planting and organic systems.
3. Natural Church Development resources. See http://www.ncd-international.org/public/.

Conclusion

We know all too well that the church in the West faces huge challenges. Os Guinness sums up what he believes is the greatest challenge the church has ever faced, with these words, "Followers of Jesus Christ confront, in the modern world, the most powerful culture in human history so far, as well as the world's first truly global culture."[150] His point is that this culture has extraordinary power to shape our lives, with consumerism in particular, out of control. As a consequence, Christian discipleship is under pressure.

In our all-pervading consumer society we encounter a giant. Consumerism and discipleship are at odds. It is simply not possible to consume one's way into discipleship. Both aim at the mastery over our lives. Who is Lord: Jesus, or the world? The starting point is not to make the church or its message suit a post-modern audience, but rather to recognise that Jesus calls us to become like him. Seeing Jesus and following him alone liberates us from bondage to ourselves and the world.

As we proclaim the "unsearchable riches of Christ" we begin to see a little of the vast glory and extent of his kingship; a kingship, which in God's time, will be all-pervading and renewing

---

[150] Os Guinness, *The Call* (Nashville, TN: Word Publishing, 1998), 57.

"as the waters cover the seas" (Isaiah 11:9). Like Jesus, it is as the people of God preach and demonstrate the gospel of the kingdom of God that disciples are made. In a world where both light and darkness, good and evil are on the increase, God's good news becomes ever more relevant and needful.

In the midst of these pressures the church needs sure theological foundations. But how effective is theology in its basic task of holding the church to biblical revelation generally, and to the truth of the gospel in particular? It is claimed that theology is stronger today than ever. In terms of academic expertise, in research and quality of publications, this is probably true.

However, more than ever we need a theology that will inspire us to explore the greatness, majesty and glory of God; a theology which will generate awe and adoration, rather than an overwhelming emphasis upon our culture and our needs. As J.I. Packer commented, when theology spawns great thoughts of man it inevitably leaves only room for small thoughts of God.[151] God occupies space as we occupy our bodies. It is as we give ourselves to magnifying God, lifting up Jesus and gratefully embracing the work of the Spirit, that the church finds fresh confidence to go into a self-obsessed world with the thought that God might be far greater than we imagine, and might have a very different agenda.

We have seen that mission is what the Bible is all about – God rescuing people and his world. It is the Bible's story, the over-arching hermeneutic of the whole of Scripture. Far from resting on one or two key texts, such as Matthew 28:18–20, it is there from beginning to end. The more we see, understand and teach this gospel coherence throughout Scripture, the better we grasp the church's purpose.

---

[151] J.I. Packer, *Knowing God* (London: Hodder & Stoughton, 2005).

Conclusion

If failing to see mission in the whole of Scripture has been an inadequacy, so also has been the tendency to focus study on the epistles at the expense of the gospels, from where we get a unique portrait of Jesus. The gospels, all in their various ways, speak incisively about mission: God's kingdom breaking into this world through the life, death and resurrection of Jesus of Nazareth. This is the bedrock of the church's calling. Paul and his writings are filled with this vision of Jesus, "I consider everything a loss compared to the surpassing greatness of knowing Christ Jesus my Lord for whose sake I have lost all things … I want to know Christ and the power of his resurrection and the fellowship of sharing in his sufferings, becoming like him in his death, and so, somehow, to attain to the resurrection from the dead" (Philippians 3:8, 10–11).

So are we optimistic or pessimistic about the church's mission and its future? To this question Lesslie Newbigin developed a stock reply, along the lines that the question shouldn't even arise because Jesus rose from the dead. It is a fact. We are not optimistic or pessimistic about facts; we can only be believing or unbelieving! It is this reality of Jesus and his kingdom, which shines over our circumstances and world and, I trust, the perspective of this book. He is God's King. It is when we lose this perspective and focus too much on the church and its performance that we swing between optimism and pessimism.

In today's world, what are the particular opportunities for the church and what should be our priorities? It is fascinating that our world – secular, urbanised, global – is strikingly similar to the Greco-Roman world. It contained multiple religious faiths, worldviews and options, the very things that live side-by-side in our society. During the Pax Romana, cities were highly connected and multi-ethnic. Since we are living in a first century-like world again, rather than the earlier context of Christendom, the missional dynamics of Jesus and the early church are very much what we need. These were dynamics which, for them, found particular expression in church planting, and from which we can all learn, today.

The priority is to keep returning to Jesus. He builds his church and he does it by making disciples. He builds from the bottom up, starting with the smallest unit, the making of a disciple. It is active and direct. Jesus lived among them, loved them and sent them into the world. From this growing number of disciples Jesus identified and developed leaders. He called them to an altogether different kind of leadership – one which served and preferred others; which gave ministry away so that all might be involved; and which released a life-giving authority, "The people were amazed at his teaching because he taught them as one who had authority, not as the teachers of the law" (Mark 1:22).

As we give intentional priority to making genuine disciples and developing Christ-like leadership, then healthy churches will follow. There are no easy answers to the practicalities of church life and mission. There is no single programme or model that alone leads to the revitalisation of Christian mission. Growth in God's kingdom is invariably "uncomfortable". It always seems to stretch us and call us away from ourselves. But in so doing, it points us to godly fruitfulness. Our greatest need is to learn afresh from the Bible, dependent on the Holy Spirit, to reveal Jesus to us. His words, his deeds and yes, his methods are what we need and they must shape everything – our lives and churches. As we do, we discover new inspiration and energy for making disciples, developing leaders, planting and equipping churches. Every church can be engaged in expressions of kingdom multiplication.

In our time more than ever God's people need to stand together. And this is what I think we see happening. A new and emerging oneness – between biblical Christians across denominations and networks, people who are uninterested in differentiating themselves from others. Rather than dwelling on secondary differences, the kingdom moves us towards "alikeness", sharing in what we have in common as followers of Jesus and spurring one another on in mission.

The history of the church is a story of grace. It recounts God's faithfulness in renewing its life and faith time and again. God is the hero; Jesus is Lord and Saviour, and the gift of the Holy Spirit has been given to the people of God. Everything is not dependent on us.

The wonder of the gospel is that our stumbling and falling are known and accepted by God. "It is not", as Richard Rohr writes, "that ... failure *might* happen, or that it will only happen to you if you are bad (which is what religious people often think) ... No, it *will* happen."[152] He continues, "The bottom line of the gospel is that most of us have to hit some kind of bottom before we even start the real journey. Up to that point, it is mostly religion. At the bottom ... you just want to breathe fresh air. The true gospel is always fresh air and spacious breathing room."[153] This is the genius of the gospel – our stumbling becomes the finding; our loss is turned into gain; dying becomes our rising. Religion sees failing as a person's record forever tainted. God sees it as an opportunity for his greatest gift. It is this message of grace that changes the world. This is

---

[152] Richard Rohr, *Falling Upwards: A Spirituality for the Two Halves of Life*, (London: SPCK, 2012), xx.
[153] Ibid., 138.

Uncomfortable Growth

to be the church's message. The more we become like Jesus of Nazareth who walked this earth, the more people will know of his transforming message and presence. It is to this kingdom life that we have been given the keys.

Index of Subjects

Bonhoeffer, Dietrich p.109–111, 115
Christendom p.26–33
Church:
    Diversity p.98f.
    Movements p.207f.
    Significance p.93
Church Planting:
    Biblical support p.100f.
    Culture p.182f.
    Methodologies p.185f.
    Multiplication p.177f.
    U.K. p.40f., 105
Culture:
    Biblical vision p.26–27
    Change p.14–17
    Secular or religious? p.22
    Trends p.17f.
Discipleship:
    Community p.136f.
    Content p.124f.
    Foundations p.111f.
    Practices of Jesus p.117f.
Gospel:
    Challenge p.86f.
    Confusions p.69f.
    Salvation p.71f.
Healing p.131f.
Holy Spirit p.75f.

Uncomfortable Growth

Islam p.24–26
Jesuits p.143–144
Kingdom of God:
    Proclaim, explain, demonstrate p.125f.
    Judgement and completion p.67f.
    Vision p.62f.
Leadership:
    Jesus p.147
    Leader-centric p.146
    Training process p.162f.
    Values p.149f.
    Vision p.153f.
Preaching p.126f.
Society:
    Modern p.34
    Post-modern p.36
    Traditional p.30
Spiritual Disciplines p.75f.
Teaching p.128f.
Transformation:
    Mission p.89f.
    Paradox p.58
    Sanctification p.73f.
Vineyard:
    Biblical doctrine p.83f.
    Church planting p.44, 204f.
    Distinctives p.45–49
    U.K. history p.43.

Bibliography

Alexander, T. Desmond. *From Eden to the New Jerusalem: Exploring God's Plan for Life on Earth.* Nottingham, UK: InterVarsity Press, 2008.

Allen, Roland. *Missionary Methods, St. Paul's or Ours?* Grand Rapids: Eerdmans, 1962.

Athanasius. *The Life of Antony & the Letter to Marcellinus.* Mahwah, NJ: Paulist Press, 1980.

Beausay, II, William. *The Leadership Genius of Jesus: Ancient Wisdom for Modern Business.* Nashville: Thomas Nelson, 1998.

Belcher, Jim. *Deep Church: A Third Way Beyond Emerging and Traditional.* Downers Grove, IL: IVP Books, 2009.

Bonaventure. *Souls Journey into God and the Life of St. Francis.* Mahwah, NJ: Paulist Press, 1978.

Bonhoeffer, Dietrich. *The Cost of Discipleship.* London: SCM Press Ltd., 1959.

_____. *Life Together: The Classic Exploration of Faith in Community.* San Francisco: Harper and Row Publishers, Inc., 1954.

Bosch, David J. *Transforming Mission: Paradigm Shifts in Theology of Mission.* Maryknoll, NY: Orbis Books, 2007.

Bruce, Alexander. B. *The Training of the Twelve: Ageless Management Principles for Developing Competent Leadership.* Grand Rapids: Kregel Publications, 1971.

Buckingham, Marcus, and Curt Coffman. *First Break All The Rules: What the World's Greatest Managers Do Differently.* London: Pocket Books, 2005.

Chang, Curtis. *Engaging Unbelief: A Captivating Strategy from

Augustine and Aquinas. Downers Grove, IL: InterVarsity Press, 2000.

Charan, Ram, Stephen Drotter, and James Noel. *The Leadership Pipeline: How to Build the Leadership Powered Company.* San Francisco: JosseyBass, 2001.

Chester, Tim. *You Can Change: God's Transforming Power for our Sinful Behaviour & Negative Emotions.* Nottingham, UK: InterVarsity Press, 2008.

Chester, Tim, and Steve Timmis. *Total Church: A Radical Reshaping Around Gospel and Community.* Nottingham, UK: InterVarsity Press, 2007.

Church of England's Mission and Public Affairs Council. *Mission-Shaped Church: Church Planting and Fresh Expressions of Church in a Changing Context.* London: Church House Publishing, 2004.

Clapp, Rodney. *A Peculiar People: The Church as Culture in a Post-Christian Society.* Downers Grove, IL: InterVarsity Press, 1996.

Clinton, J. Robert. *The Making of a Leader.* Colorado Springs, CO: NavPress, 1988.

Cole, Neil. *Cultivating a Life for God: Multiplying Disciples through Life Transformation Groups.* Carol Stream, IL: ChurchSmart Resources, 1999.

_____. *Organic Church: Growing Faith Where Life Happens.* San Francisco: Jossey-Bass, 2005.

Crouch, Andy. *Culture Making: Recovering Our Creative Calling.* Downers Grove, IL: InterVarsity Press, 2008.

De Young, Kevin, and Ted Kluck. *Why We Love the Church: In Praise of Institutions and Organized Religion.* Chicago, IL: Moody Publishers, 2009.

Drane, John. *Faith in a Changing Culture.* Vol. London: Marshal Pickering, 1997.

Easum, William M. *Sacred Cow Makes Gourmet Burgers.* Nashville: Abingdon, 1995.

Fee, Gordon. *Paul, the Spirit and the People of God.* London: Hodder and Stoughton, 1997.

Ferguson, Niall. *Civilization: The West and the Rest.* London: Penguin Books, 2011.

Frost, Michael, and Alan Hirsch. *The Shaping of Things to Come: Innovation and Mission for the 21st-Century Church.* Peabody, MA: Hendrickson Publishers, 2003.

Gibbs, Eddie. *In Name Only: Tackling the Problem of Nominal Christianity.* Pasadena, CA: Fuller Seminary Press, 1994.

Gibbs, Eddie, and Ryan K. Bolger. *Emerging Churches: Creating Christian Community in Postmodern Cultures.* London: SPCK, 2006.

Gibbs, Eddie, and Ian Coffey. *Church Next: Quantum Changes in Christian Ministry.* Leicester, England: InterVarsity Press, 2001.

Goleman, Daniel. *The New Leaders: Transforming the Art of Leadership into the Science of Results.* New York: Time Warner, 2003.

Guder, Darrell L. *The Continuing Conversion of the Church.* Grand Rapids: Eerdmans, 2000.

Guiness, Os. *The Call.* Nashville: Word Books, 1998.

Hauerwas, Stanley, and William H. Willimon. *Resident Aliens – Life in the Christian Colony: A Provocative Christian Assessment of Culture and Ministry for People Who Know that Something Is Wrong.* Nashville: Abingdon Press, 1989.

Hendricks, Howard, and William Hendricks. *As Iron Sharpens Iron: Building Character in a Mentoring Relationship.* Chicago: Moody Press, 1995.

Hiebert, Paul. *Missiological Implications of Epistemological Shifts – Affirming Truth in a Modern/Postmodern World.* Harrisburg, PA: Trinity Press, 1999.

Hirsch, Alan. *The Forgotten Ways: Reactivating the Missional Church.* Grand Rapids: Brazos Press, 2006.

Ignatius, Loyola. *The Spiritual Exercises of St. Ignatius.* Translated by Anthony Mattola. New York: Bantam Doubleday Dell, 1989.

Jackson, Bill. *The Quest for the Radical Middle: A History of the Vineyard.* Cape Town, South Africa: Vineyard International Publishing, 1999.

Jenkins, Philip. *The Next Christendom: The Coming of Global Christianity.* Oxford: Oxford University Press, 2002.

Keller, Timothy. *Center Church: Doing Balanced, Gospel-Centered Ministry in Your City.* Grand Rapids, MI: Zondervan, 2012.

_____. *The Reason for God: Belief in an Age of Scepticism.* London: Hodder & Stoughton, 2008,

Lewis, C.S. *The Weight of Glory.* New York: Simon & Schuster, 1949.

Livermore, David A. *Leading with Cultural Intelligence: The New Secret to Success.* New York: Amacom Books, 2010.

_____. *Serving with Eyes Wide Open: Doing Short-Term Missions with Cultural Intellgence.* Grand Rapids, MI: Baker Books, 2006.

Logan, Bob, and Sherlyn Carlton. *Coaching 101.* St. Charles, IL: ChurchSmart Publishing, 2003.

Lowney, Chris. *Heroic Leadership: Best Practices from a 450-Year-Old Company that Changed the World.* Chicago: Loyola Press, 2003.

Marshall, Colin, and Tony Payne. *The Trellis And The Vine: The*

Ministry Mind-Shift that Changes Everything. Sydney: Matthias Media, 2009.

McCall, Morgan W. *High Flyers: Developing the Next Generation of Leaders.* Boston: Harvard Business School Press, 1998.

McGrath, Alister E. *The Future of Christianity.* Oxford: Blackwell Publishers Limited, 2002.

————. *Evangelicalism and the Future of Christianity.* London: Hodder & Stoughton, 1996.

McManus, Erwin Raphael. *An Unstoppable Force: Daring to Become the Church God Had in Mind.* Orange, CA: Yates & Yates, 2001.

McNeal, Reggie. *Revolution in Leadership.* Nashville: Abingdon, 1998.

Merton, Thomas. *The Wisdom of the Desert.* New York: New Directions Publishing, 1970.

Metaxas, Eric. *Bonhoeffer, Pastor, Martyr, Prophet, Spy.* Nashville, TN: Thomas Nelson, 2010.

Morphew, Derek. *Breakthrough: Discovering the Kingdom.* Cape Town: Vineyard International Publishing, 2007.

Murray, Stuart. *Church Planting: Laying Foundations.* Carlisle, Cumbria: Paternoster Press, 1998.

Newbigin, Lesslie. *The Gospel in a Pluralistic Society.* London: SPCK, 1989.

Newbigin, Lesslie, compiled and introduced by Paul Weston. *Lesslie Newbigin: Missionary Theologian: A Reader.* London: SPCK, 2006.

Nouwen, Henri, J.M. *Creative Ministry.* New York: Bantam Doubleday Dell, 1978.

————. *The Way of the Heart: Desert Spirituality and Contemporary Ministry.* San Francisco: Harper Collins, 1991.

_____. *The Wounded Healer.* Garden City, NY: Image/Doubleday, 1979.

Quinn, Robert E. *Deep Change.* San Francisco: Jossey-Bass, 1996.

Riddell, Peter G., and Peter Cotterell. *Islam in Context: Past, Present and Future.* Grand Rapids: Baker Academic, 2003.

Robinson, Martin. *Planting Mission Shaped Churches Today.* Oxford: Monarch Books, 2006.

Robinson, Martin, and Dwight Smith. *Invading Secular Space: Strategies for Tomorrow's Church.* London: Monarch Books, 2003.

Rohr, Richard. *Jesus' Plan for a New World: The Sermon on the Mount.* Cincinnati, OH: St. Anthony Messenger Press, 1996.

_____. *Falling Upwards: A Spirituality for the Two Halves of Life.* London: SPCK, 2012.

Roxburgh, Alan J. *The Missionary Congregation, Leadership, and Liminality: Christian Mission and Modern Culture.* Harrisburg, PA: Trinity Press International, 1997.

Schaller, Lyle E. *Discontinuity and Hope – Radical Change and the Path to the Future.* Nashville: Abingdon, 1999.

Schwarz, Christian A. *Natural Church Development: A Guide to Eight Essential Qualities of Healthy Churches.* Carol Stream, IL: Church Smart Resources, 1996.

Smith, James K.A. *Desiring the Kingdom: Worship, Worldview, and Cultural Formation.* Grand Rapids, MI: Baker Academic, 2009.

Spencer, Nick, and Robert White. *Christianity, Climate Change and Sustainable Living.* London: SPCK, 2007.

Sweet, Leonard. *Aqua Church: Essential Leadership Arts for Piloting Your Church in Today's Fluid Culture.* Loveland,

CO: Group Publishing Inc., 1999.
Thomas, Viv. *Future Leader.* Milton Keynes, UK: Paternoster, 1999.
Wheatley, Margaret J. *Leadership and the New Science: Discovering Order in a Chaotic World.* San Francisco: Berrett-Koehler Publishers, 1999.
Willard, Dallas. *The Divine Conspiracy: Rediscovering Our Hidden Life in God.* London: Fount Paperbacks, Harper Collins Publishers, 1998.
―――――. *Hearing God: Building an Intimate Relationship with the Creator.* London: Fount, 1999.
―――――. *Renovation of the Heart: Putting on the Character of Christ.* Colorado Springs: NavPress, 2002.
―――――. *The Spirit of the Disciplines: Understanding How God Changes Lives.* London: Hodder and Stoughton, 1996.
Wright, Christopher J.H. *The Mission of God: Unlocking the Bible's Grand Narrative.* Nottingham, UK: Inter-Varsity Press, 2006.
Wright, N.T. *The Challenge of Jesus.* London: SPCK, 2000.
Wright, Tom. *How God Became King: Getting to the Heart of the Gospels.* London: SPCK, 2012.
―――――. *Surprised by Hope.* London: SPCK, 2007.
―――――. *Virtue Reborn.* London: SPCK, 2010.
Wright, Walter C. *Relational Leadership: A Biblical Model for Influence and Service.* Downers Grove, IL, 2009.
Yancey, George. *One Body, One Spirit: Principles of Successful Multiracial Churches.* Downers Grove, IL: InterVarsity Press, 2003.

Made in the USA
Charleston, SC
18 May 2015